Studies in Geometry Series

Proofs
Workbook

Reasoning with Mathematics

Tammy Pelli

GARLIC PRESS

Educational Materials for Teachers and Parents

899 South College Mall Road
Bloomington, IN 47401

www.garlicpress.com

© 2004 by Stanley H. Collins
Revised printing 2007
All rights strictly reserved.

ISBN 978-1-930820-46-3

Table of Contents

Introduction
About This Workbook   1

Chapter 1   What Is a Proof?
Getting Started   3

Chapter 2   Strategy #1
Everything You Need to Know   5

Chapter 3   Strategy #2
Develop Lines of Reasoning   11

Chapter 4   Strategy #3
Work Backward   15

Chapter 5   Strategy #4
Paragraph Proofs   17

Chapter 6   Strategy #5
Creating Order   25

Chapter 7   Strategy #6
Formal Proofs   31

Glossary
Potential Reasons/Justifications   39

Answer Key   45

Introduction

- The concepts that are studied and applied in a geometry course fall into two categories: theorems and postulates. Theorems are generalizations that cannot be assumed true without proof, while postulates are generalizations that can be accepted as true without proof. Postulates along with established definitions help to establish the broader realm of theorems and expand our variety of geometrical relationships.

- This workbook will provide an opportunity to develop specific skills used in proof writing. Each strategy develops a particular technique that can be used when writing a proof.

- Because every textbook is different, reference to specific theorems and postulates is not made overtly so that this workbook can complement a student's study of geometry without conflicting with his/her schoolwork.

- This workbook requires a knowledge of basic geometry. It is intended to be used after a student has studied most, if not all, of the topics in a typical geometry course. It can serve as a review of topics as well as helping students to develop the skills they need to write proofs.

- A Glossary at the back of the workbook provides a thorough list of all definitions, postulates, and theorems which are used throughout the workbook.

- The Answer Key provides answers to all practice exercises. In some cases, there are multiple ways to correctly complete an exercise. In those cases, it is indicated in the Answer Key that there could be other correct proofs. Also, there are no answers provided for the last set of proofs in the workbook. This is because the goal of that activity is for the student to create as many conceivable possible proofs as possible.

Chapter 1

What Is a Proof?

What is a proof? A proof is a mathematical argument. It begins with a specific set of given information. Then a series of steps leads to the desired conclusions. A proof can be written as a paragraph or in a 2-column form. Proofs include mathematical statements and the justifications for those statements in the form of definitions, postulates, theorems, or properties.

How long are they? A proof can have 2 steps or over a hundred steps depending on the complexity of the conclusion being developed and how direct a route the writer takes to reach the conclusion. Proofs in this workbook will typically range from 3 to 8 steps.

How do I know when I'm done? A proof is finished when you have stated the conclusion and when each step you have stated previous to the conclusion is logically derived from the step before it or from a piece of given information.

What do they look like? Formal proofs (2-column proofs) are organized in T-charts. On the left is a numbered list of mathematical statements (often either referred to as the statements or the conclusions). On the right is a numbered list of properties, definitions, theorems, and/or postulates that defend each of the statements (often called either reasons or justifications). Paragraph proofs contain the same information as a formal proof, but they are organized into sentences as in a normal paragraph.

If I could just get started... Knowing where to begin a proof can be the toughest part. Thinking that you must have the entire plan for the proof in your mind before you can begin is even worse. This workbook will take you through a variety of exercises to help you develop strategies to write proofs successfully.

Building up to writing a proof... Instead of jumping right in to writing proofs, this workbook will first give you the opportunity to practice the logical thinking skills used in proof writing. Once you have developed your reasoning skills and can piece information together, you will move on to organizing and to writing proofs. Follow these strategies to form your basic plan.

Strategy #1 Write down everything you know based on the givens and the figure.
Strategy #2 Develop lines of reasoning.
Strategy #3 Work backward.
Strategy #4 Paragraph proofs.
Strategy #5 Creating order.
Strategy #6 Formal proofs.

What do I need to know to get started? Writing proofs requires a basic knowledge of geometrical vocabulary and relationships. A list of important definitions, postulates and theorems is at the back of this workbook for your aid. Your own textbook probably has a list of vocabulary, postulates, theorems, and properties to which you can also refer for help in solving the exercises in this workbook. Keep in mind that the wording of theorems, etc., might be a bit different from book to book.

Helpful hints: If you're writing a proof and you feel stuck, go back to Strategy #1. Brainstorming everything you know about a situation will almost always give you options to use. Drawing on the picture often helps to understand given information. Other times it may help to take the picture apart (redraw just a part of the picture and focus on it).

Chapter 2

Strategy #1

Strategy #1 Write down everything you know based on the givens and the figure.

✓ When you are writing a proof, whether it is a formal proof or a paragraph proof, you will end with a series of statements and their mathematical justifications in a logically ordered list. But it is often too difficult to come up with all the statements, all the reasons, and all of the organization all at the same time.

✓ This section is devoted to developing ideas. We won't worry about what order things should be in. We just want to get our minds working and discover how much we know about different geometrical situations.

✓ When you are asked to write a proof, you are given something to start with and something you are asked to prove based on the given information. Here we are not going to worry about trying to prove anything in particular. We are going to develop as many ideas as possible about each set of information.

For Example *Write everything you know based on the given information and the figure.*
Given: *ABCD* is a trapezoid.

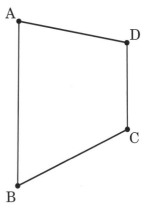

- A trapezoid is defined as a quadrilateral with one pair of sides that is parallel and one pair of sides that is not parallel: *ABCD* is a quadrilateral, $\overline{AB} \| \overline{DC}$.
- Since $\overline{AB} \| \overline{DC}$, everything that we know about parallel lines which are cut by a transversal can be applied… $m\angle BAD + m\angle CDA = 180°$ and $\angle B$ and $\angle C$ are also supplementary because same side interior angles are supplementary.
- Since ABCD is a quadrilateral, $m\angle A + m\angle B + m\angle C + m\angle D = 360°$ because the sum of the interior angles of a quadrilateral is always 360°.

For Example *Write everything you know based on the given information and the figure.*
Given: *EFGHIJKL* is a regular octagon.
- A regular polygon is a convex polygon that is equilateral and equiangular, so *EFGHIJKL* is equilateral and equiangular.
- Equiangular means that all of the angles are congruent, so
  $\angle E \cong \angle F \cong \angle G \cong \angle H \cong \angle I \cong \angle J \cong \angle K \cong \angle L.$
- Equilateral means that all of the sides are congruent,
  so $\overline{EF} \cong \overline{FG} \cong \overline{GH} \cong \overline{HI} \cong \overline{IJ} \cong \overline{JK} \cong \overline{KL} \cong \overline{LE}.$

- In a convex polygon, the sum of the interior angles is $(n-2)180°$, where n is the number of sides. The sum of the interior angles for this octagon is 1080°.
- If there are 1080° in this octagon, and all of the 8 angles are congruent, then each angle is 135°.
- The number of diagonals in a polygon is found using the formula $\frac{1}{2}n(n-3)$ where n is the number of sides. There are 20 diagonals that can be drawn in this octagon.

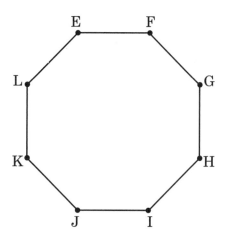

Practice *Write everything you know based on the given information and the figure.*

1. Given: *UMIO* is a rhombus.

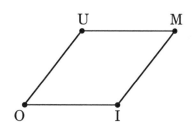

2. Given: ΔWYL is an isosceles triangle with a base of $\overline{LY}$.

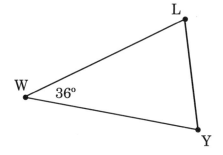

3. Given: $\overleftrightarrow{XH} \parallel \overleftrightarrow{EQ}$.

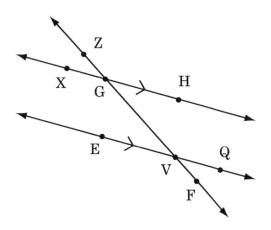

4. Given: $\angle NPA$ is a right angle.

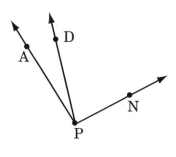

5. Given: $\overrightarrow{BJ}$ is an angle bisector.

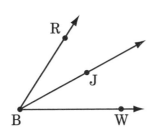

6. Given: *OBIQPD* is a hexagon.

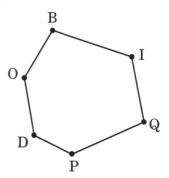

7. Given: *TYGH* is a square.

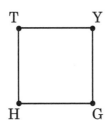

8. Given: $\overline{SF}$ an altitude.

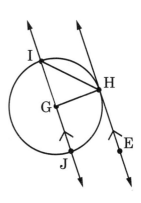

• Often there are several given statements, instead of just one. Therefore your brainstorming (writing everything you know) from the given statement must follow each of the statements individually. In doing so, you must try to develop connections between the given statements.

For Example

Given: $\odot G$ has tangent $\overleftrightarrow{HE}$ and $\overleftrightarrow{IJ} \parallel \overleftrightarrow{HE}$.

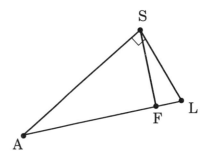

- A circle is a set of points that is equidistant from the center. Therefore *I*, *H* and *J* are equidistant from *G*.
- A circle is named for its center, so *G* is the center of this circle.
- *E* is not a point on the circle.
- A chord is a segment with endpoints on a circle: $\overline{IJ}$ and $\overline{IH}$ are chords.
- A diameter is a chord which passes through the center of the circle: $\overline{IJ}$ is the diameter of this circle.
- A radius is a segment with an endpoint at the center of a circle and an endpoint on the circle: $\overline{IG}$, $\overline{GH}$, $\overline{GJ}$ are all radii.
- All radii of a circle are congruent: $\overline{IG} \cong \overline{GH} \cong \overline{GJ}$.

- Since $\overline{IG} \cong \overline{GH}$, ΔIGH is an isosceles triangle.
- A point of tangency is a point at which a tangent line intersects a circle: H is a point of tangency.
- $\overleftrightarrow{HE} \perp \overline{GH}$ because a tangent line is perpendicular to the radius drawn to the point of tangency.

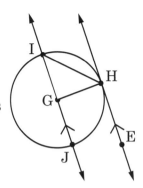

- Since $\overleftrightarrow{HE} \perp \overline{GH}$, $\angle GHE$ and its supplement are both right angles with measures of 90° as we know from the definitions of perpendicular lines and right angles.
- $\overleftrightarrow{IJ} \parallel \overleftrightarrow{HE}$ When parallel lines are cut by a transversal (in this case the transversal would be $\overline{GH}$), alternate interior angles are congruent. So since $\angle GHE$ is a right angle, so is $\angle IGH$.
- If two lines intersect to form right angles, then they are perpendicular: $\overline{GH} \perp \overleftrightarrow{IJ}$.
- Since $\angle IGH$ is a right angle, ΔIGH is a right triangle.
- Since ΔIGH is a right isosceles triangle, it is a 45–45–90 triangle and $IH = IG\sqrt{2} = GH\sqrt{2}$.
- $\overarc{IHJ}$ is a semicircle with a measure of 180°, from the definition of a semicircle.
- $\overarc{IH}$ and $\overarc{HJ}$ are minor arcs, from the definition of a minor arc. $\overarc{IJH}$ and $\overarc{HIJ}$ are major arcs, based on the definition of a major arc.
- $\angle IGH \cong \angle HGJ$ because both are right angles and all right angles measure 90°.
- $\angle IGH$ and $\angle HGJ$ are both central angles, from the definition of a central angle.

✓ This is a long list of statements and their justifications. There are other statements, some of which are closely related to those stated, which could also be made. It is unlikely that all of these would be needed in a single proof. However, it is likely that some of these would be needed. When it comes time to write proofs, the task will focus on determining which pieces of information are relevant to the goal of what is to be proven.

Practice *Write everything you know based on the given information and the figure.*

1. Given: $\overline{AB} \cong \overline{EF}$ and $\overline{AG} \cong \overline{HF}$.

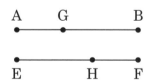

2. Given: $\overrightarrow{QR} \perp \overrightarrow{QP}$.
$m\angle TQR + m\angle SQP = 90°$.

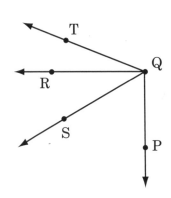

3. Given: $\overline{CG} \perp \overline{AE}$.
I is the midpoint of $\overline{AE}$.

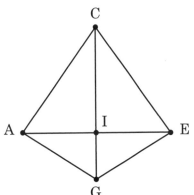

4. Given: $\triangle JNO$ is equiangular.
$LKOM$ is a parallelogram.

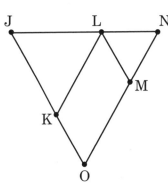

5. Given: $\angle BAD \cong \angle DBA$ and $\overline{AC} \cong \overline{BC}$.

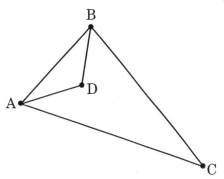

6. Given: $RTSU$ is a parallelogram.
$m\angle RTS = 53°$.

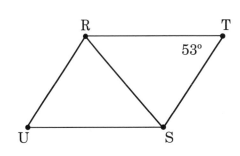

Chapter 3

Strategy #2

Develop Lines of Reasoning

Strategy #2 Develop ideas into lines of reasoning.

✓ Brainstorming starts our minds working on a proof. But proofs require a logical argument, not just a randomly ordered list of ideas. Our goal in this section is to develop lines of reasoning.

✓ A line of reasoning starts with a fact. Another statement can follow that is based on the first fact. If possible, another statement can follow based on the second statement. At each stage, a reason needs to be given to support the statement.

✓ After each statement you write, ask yourself, "What can I conclude from my statement?" Keep asking until you reach a dead end. After you end a line of reasoning, go back to the picture and start with a different piece of information. You might even be able to develop a totally different line of reasoning if you think about the fact differently.

✓ This is related to the brainstorming in Strategy #1. The difference is that we are going to brainstorm in a logical way.

For Example *Develop as many lines of reasoning as possible based on this picture.*

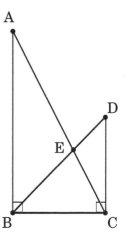

Line 1: • ∠*ABC* and ∠*DCB* are right angles; given.
- Δ*ABC* and Δ*BCD* are right triangles; definition of a right triangle.
- ∠*A* and ∠*ACB* are complementary and ∠*D* and ∠*DBC* are complementary; the acute angles of a right triangle are complementary.
- $m\angle A + m\angle ACB = 90°$ and $m\angle D + m\angle DBC = 90°$; definition of complementary angles.

Line 2: • ∠*ABC* and ∠*DCB* are right angles; given.
- Δ*ABC* and Δ*BCD* are right triangles; definition of a right triangle.
- ∠*A* and ∠*ACB* are complementary and ∠*D* and ∠*DBC* are complementary; the acute angles of a right triangle are complementary.
- ∠*A*, ∠*ACB*, ∠*D*, ∠*DBC* are less than 90°; definition of acute angles.

Line 3: • ∠*ABC* and ∠*DCB* are right angles; given.
- $\overline{AB} \perp \overline{BC}$ and $\overline{DC} \perp \overline{BC}$; two lines are perpendicular if and only if they intersect to form right angles.
- $\overline{AB} \parallel \overline{DC}$; if two lines are perpendicular to the same line, they are parallel.
- ∠*A* ≅ ∠*ACD* and ∠*ABD* ≅ ∠*D*; alternate interior angles are congruent.

Line 4: • ∠*ABC* and ∠*DCB* are right angles; given.
- $\overline{AB} \perp \overline{BC}$ and $\overline{DC} \perp \overline{BC}$; two lines are perpendicular if and only if they intersect to form right angles.
- $\overline{AB} \parallel \overline{DC}$; if two lines are perpendicular to the same line then, they are parallel.
- ∠*ABC* and ∠*DCB* are supplementary; same-side interior angles are supplementary.
- $m\angle ABC + m\angle DCB = 180°$; definition of supplementary angles.

Line 5: • ∠*ABC* and ∠*DCB* are right angles; given.
- $m\angle ABC = 90° = m\angle DCB$; definition of right angles.

Line 6: • ∠*AEB* ≅ ∠*DEC*; vertical angles are congruent.

Practice *Develop as many lines of reasoning as possible based on each figure.*

1. Given: $\overleftrightarrow{AB} \parallel \overleftrightarrow{CD}$, $\overleftrightarrow{BD} \perp \overleftrightarrow{CD}$.

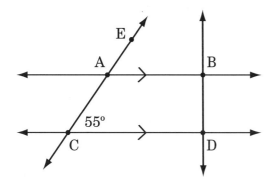

2. Given: *G* and *I* are midpoints.

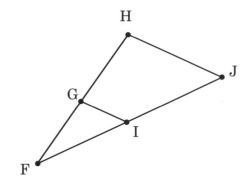

3. Given: *MNOP* and *PQRS* are parallelograms.

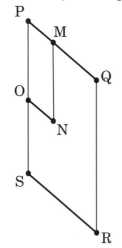

4. Given: *VZXY* is a rhombus.

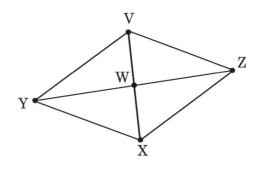

5. Given: ΔIWR and ΔWYI are right triangles with hypotenuses $\overline{IR}$ and $\overline{WI}$.

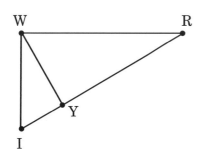

6. Given: $\overline{ED} \parallel \overline{BC}$.

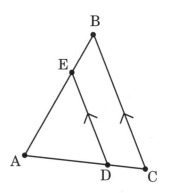

✓ Once you have learned to develop lines of reasoning, you can move to combining lines of reasoning. Some proofs you will write later require just one line of reasoning. More advanced proofs require a combination of reasons to arrive at a final answer. That is what you will prepare for here.

For Example *Develop as many lines of reasoning as possible based on this picture of parallelogram FXWK.*

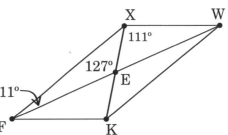

✓ Start with the same approach you've been practicing.

Line 1: *FXWK* is a parallelogram; given.
- $\overline{XW} \parallel \overline{FK}$; definition of a parallelogram.
- $\angle WXK \cong \angle XKF$; alternate interior angles are congruent.
- $m \angle WXK = 111° = m \angle XKF$; given and by substitution.

Line 2: *FXWK* is a parallelogram; given.
- $\overline{FX} \parallel \overline{KW}$; definition of a parallelogram.
- $\angle XWF \cong \angle KFW$; alternate interior angles are congruent.

Line 3: $m \angle FEX = 127°$; given.
- $\angle FEX$ and $\angle XEW$ are supplementary (2 angles forming a straight angle are supplementary).
- $m \angle FEX + m \angle XEW = 180°$; definition of supplementary angles.
- $127° + m \angle XEW = 180°$; substitution.
- $m \angle XEW = 53°$; subtraction.
- $m \angle XEW + m \angle EXW + m \angle XWE = 180°$; the sum of the interior angles of a triangle is 180°.
- $m \angle EXW = 111°$; given.
- $53° + 111° + m \angle XWE = 180°$; substitution.
- $m \angle XWE = 16°$; subtraction.

Line 4: *FXWK* is a parallelogram; given.
- $\overline{FX} \cong \overline{KW}$ and $\overline{XW} \cong \overline{FK}$; opposite sides of a parallelogram are congruent.

Line 5: *FXWK* is a parallelogram; given.
- *E* is the midpoint of $\overline{XK}$ and $\overline{FW}$; the diagonals of a parallelogram bisect each other.
- $\overline{FE} \cong \overline{EW}$ and $\overline{XE} \cong \overline{EK}$; definition of a midpoint.

✓ There are multiple ways to end a single line of reasoning. Another way to go with Line 3 follows.

Line 6: $m \angle FEX = 127°$; given.
- $\angle FEX$ and $\angle XEW$ are supplementary (2 angles forming a straight angle are supplementary).
- $m \angle FEX + m \angle XEW = 180°$; definition of supplementary angles.
- $127° + m \angle XEW = 180°$; substitution.
- $m \angle XEW = 53°$; subtraction.
- $m \angle XEW = 53° = m \angle FEK$; vertical angles are congruent and substitution.

✓ Sometimes you can combine lines of reasoning to create new ones. Take the thinking from a couple of lines of reasoning that you have already created and see what happens if you combine them.
✓ *Helpful hint:* It is often helpful to redraw a picture to include only the information relating to the line of reasoning you are developing.

Line 7: Line 5 + Line 4: $\Delta FEX \cong \Delta WEK$ and $\Delta FEK \cong \Delta WEX$; SSS. (If three sides of one triangle are congruent to three sides of another triangle, then the triangles are congruent.)

Line 8: Line 2 + Line 3: $m \angle XWE = 16° = m \angle EFK$; alternate interior angles are congruent.

Line 9: Line 6 + Line 5: $\Delta FEK \cong \Delta WEX$; SAS. (If two sides and the included angle of one triangle are congruent to two sides and the included angle of another triangle, the triangles are congruent.)

Line 10: Line 1 + Line 8 + Line 4: $\Delta FEK \cong \Delta WEX$; ASA. (If two angles and the included side of one triangle are congruent to two angles and the included side of another triangle, the triangles are congruent.)

Practice *Develop as many lines of reasoning as possible based on each figure. Include combined lines of reasoning.*

1. Given: ∠*BAC* ≅ ∠*EAD*.

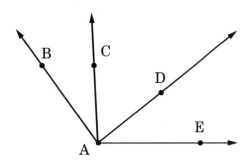

2. Given: *NKLM* is a square.

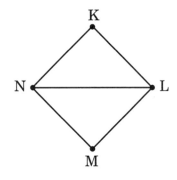

3. Given: *X* and *U* are midpoints.
$\overline{YZ} \parallel \overline{WV}$.

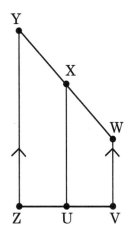

4. Given: $\overline{DE} \parallel \overline{CB}$.

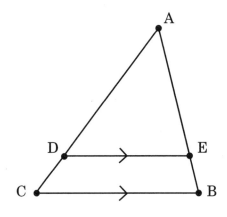

5. Given: $\overline{DE} \perp \overline{CE}$, *FE* = *DE*.

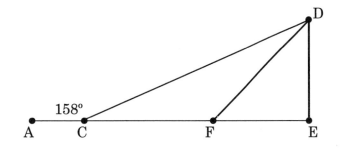

6. Given: $\overline{GH} \parallel \overline{IJ}$.

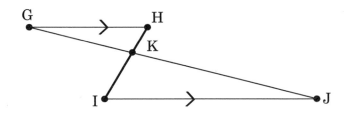

Strategy #3

Strategy #3 Work backward from the statement to be proved.

✓ So far we have simply brainstormed everything we know about a particular situation. We can narrow our list by brainstorming with our goal in mind.

✓ In this section, instead of starting with given information, we're going to start with the statement we must prove. As we look at the statement to be proved, we'll ask ourselves what we would need to know in order to make that statement.

✓ Below are three examples based on this one picture. In each case, we have thought backward from the proof. We have tried to determine what would have to be given, or what we would need to be able to determine, before we could make the statement we are trying to prove.

For Example

Prove: $\angle PEL \cong \angle EJB$.

These angles look like corresponding angles. If we knew that $\overleftrightarrow{ML}$ was parallel to $\overleftrightarrow{KB}$, then we'd be able to say that $\angle PEL \cong \angle EJB$ because when 2 parallel lines are cut by a transversal, then corresponding angles are congruent.

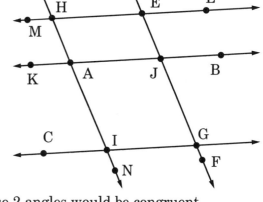

Prove: $\angle OHM \cong \angle NIG$.

These angles aren't vertical angles or corresponding angles, so we need to look for some sort of extended relationship between them. But $\angle OHM$ looks like it is a corresponding angle to $\angle CIA$. If $\overleftrightarrow{ML} \parallel \overleftrightarrow{CG}$, then those 2 angles would be congruent. $\angle CIA$ is congruent to $\angle NIG$ because they are vertical angles. So we would be able to say that $\angle OHM \cong \angle NIG$ by the transitive property.

Prove: $AIGJ$ is a parallelogram.

One way to prove that a quadrilateral is a parallelogram is to prove that both pairs of opposite sides are parallel. If we knew that $\overleftrightarrow{KB} \parallel \overleftrightarrow{CG}$ and that $\overleftrightarrow{ON} \parallel \overleftrightarrow{PF}$, then we would be able to conclude that this is a parallelogram.

Another way to prove that a quadrilateral is a parallelogram is if you know that the opposite angles are congruent. So we could do this proof if we knew (or had a way to determine) that $\angle JAI \cong \angle IGJ$ and $\angle AIG \cong \angle GJA$.

Practice *Think backward to determine what would have to be given or determined before you could make the following "Prove" statements. Also explain why you would need those pieces of information.*

1. Prove: $RS = \frac{1}{2}UV$.

2. Prove: $\triangle TRS \sim \triangle TUV$.

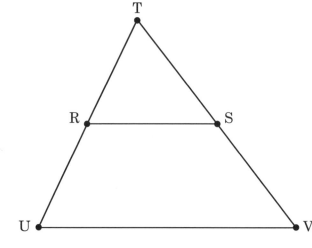

3. Prove: $ILJK$ is a parallelogram.

4. Prove: $\triangle KIL \cong \triangle LJK$.

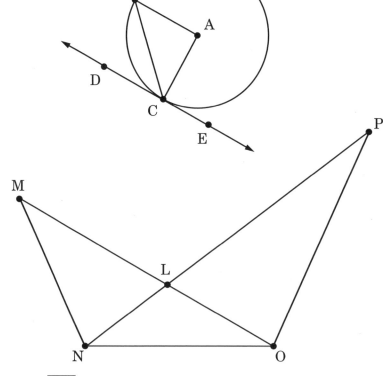

5. Prove: $\overleftrightarrow{DE}$ is tangent to $\odot A$.

6. Prove: $\triangle ABC$ is 45–45–90 triangle.

7. Prove: $\triangle MNO \sim \triangle NOP$.

8. Prove: $\angle M \cong \angle P$.

Chapter 5

Strategy #4

Strategy #4 Writing proofs in paragraph form.

✓ Using Strategy #1 will give you a long list of information. Some of that information is probably necessary for the proof and some of it will probably not be included in the final proof. The more proofs you write, the better you will get at realizing what is important in the brainstorming phase, and what isn't. Strategy #1 is good to get started. It helps to assemble most of what you need for your proof right in front of you. Then, writing the actual proof is just about putting what you already know into logical order.

✓ Combining Strategy #2 and Strategy #3 creates a proof. When writing a proof, you need to develop lines of reasoning that are aimed at reaching the conclusion you're trying to prove. Strategy #4 is the first stage in solid proof writing.

✓ This section is devoted to writing proofs in paragraph form. It is really like putting your exact thoughts on paper. It is an informal format for writing proofs. It includes both mathematical statements and their justifications.

For Example

Write a paragraph proof.
Given: $\overline{WV}$ is the median of trapezoid *TXYU*.
Prove: $\overline{WV} \parallel \overline{TU}$.

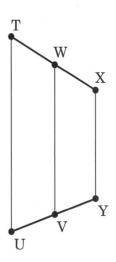

First, think through what information you are given.
Since this is a trapezoid, the bases are parallel, so $\overline{TU} \parallel \overline{XY}$. That information seems related to what is to be proved, but doesn't lead to it directly. The median of a trapezoid is a segment which connects the midpoints of the legs. The definition of a median doesn't seem particularly helpful, but there is another fact about the median which might be helpful: The median of a trapezoid is parallel to the bases. Since the statement to be proved involved the median being parallel to one of the bases, this seems to be the key to the proof.

Second, organize only the important information into a proof in paragraph form.
Remember to include the reasons for the statements. Always begin with the given information.
$\overline{WV}$ is the median of trapezoid *TXYU*. A median of a trapezoid is parallel to the bases of the trapezoid, so $\overline{WV} \parallel \overline{TU}$.

For Example *Write a paragraph proof.*
Given: ∆EBD is inscribed in ⊙A.
Prove: m ∠DBE = 90°.

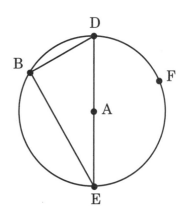

First, think through what information you are given.
Since ∆EBD is inscribed in ⊙A, ∠DBE is an inscribed angle. Our proof deals with the measure of that inscribed angle. The rule for finding the measure of an inscribed angle states that the measure of an inscribed angle is equal to half the measure of its intercepted arc. The endpoints of the angle are on a diameter, as we can see from the figure. Thus, the angle intercepts an arc which is a semicircle named $\overparen{EFD}$. The measure of a semicircle is 180°, and half of 180° is 90°, so we have found the bridge between the given and what is to be proved.

Second, organize only the important information into a proof in paragraph form. *Remember to include the reasons for the statements. Always begin with the given information.*
We can see from the figure that $\overline{ED}$ is a diameter because it is a chord which passes through the center of the circle. Since $\overparen{EFD}$ is an arc with its endpoints on the diameter, it is a semicircle based on the definition of a diameter. The measure of any semicircle is 180°, based on the definition of a semicircle. It is given that ∆EBD is inscribed in ⊙A. Since ∆EBD is inscribed, so is ∠EBD. The arc intercepted by that inscribed angle is $\overparen{EBD}$. Therefore the $m \angle EBD = \frac{1}{2} m \overparen{EFD} = \frac{1}{2}(180°) = 90°$, because the measure of an inscribed angle is always half of the measure of its intercepted arc.

In fact, using the same thinking, there is a different way to finish this proof: We can see from the figure that $\overline{ED}$ is a diameter because it is a chord which passes through the center of the circle. Since $\overparen{EBD}$ is an arc with its endpoints being the endpoints of a diameter, it is a semicircle based on the definition of a diameter. The measure of any semicircle is 180°, based on the definition of a semicircle. It is given that ∆EBD is inscribed in ⊙A. Since ∆EBD is inscribed, so is ∠EBD. In fact ∠EBD is inscribed in semicircle $\overparen{EBD}$. An angle inscribed in a semicircle is a right angle, so ∠EBD is a right angle. By the definition of a right angle, the $m \angle EBD = 90°$.

Practice *Write a paragraph proof after working Strategy #2 and Strategy #3 to develop the thinking behind the proof.*

1. Given: $m \angle UZA + m \angle WAZ = 180°$.
   Prove: $\overleftrightarrow{TZ} \parallel \overleftrightarrow{AW}$.

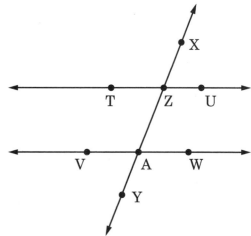

2. Given: $\triangle GKH \cong \triangle JKI$.
  Prove: $\overline{GH} \parallel \overline{IJ}$.

3. Given: $\angle OQL \cong \angle SRP$.
  Prove: $\overleftrightarrow{LM} \parallel \overleftrightarrow{NS}$.

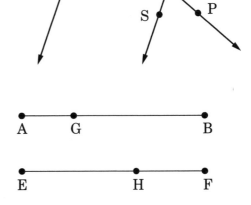

4. Given: $\overline{AB} \cong \overline{EF}$ and $\overline{AG} \cong \overline{HF}$.
  Prove: $\overline{GB} \cong \overline{EH}$.

5. Given: $\overleftrightarrow{QR} \perp \overrightarrow{QP}$.
        $m\angle TQR + m\angle SQP = 90°$.
  Prove: $m\angle TQR = m\angle RQS$.

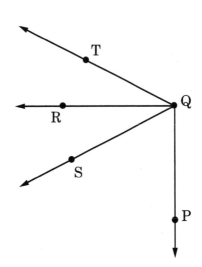

✓ Proofs are not always the result of a direct connection between the given and what is to be proved. Sometimes you need to think from both the beginning and the end to understand where the given and the prove meet in the middle.

For Example *Write a paragraph proof.*
Given: *DEFG* is a trapezoid.
       DJ = JE and *GK = KF.*
Prove: ∠*D* is supplementary to ∠*DJK.*

First, think through what information you are given.
∠*D* and ∠*DJK* look like same-side interior angles. They would be supplementary if $\overline{DG}$ was parallel to $\overline{JK}$. $\overline{DG}$ would be parallel to $\overline{JK}$ if $\overline{JK}$ was a median of the trapezoid. The given information says that *DJ = JE* and *GK = KF*, which would make *J* and *K* the midpoints of the legs. Since a median is defined to be the segment which connects the midpoints of the legs of a trapezoid, we know that $\overline{JK}$ is the median, which is the piece of information we needed to connect givens to the prove.

Second, organize the information into a proof in paragraph form. *Remember to include the reasons for the statements.* It is given that *DJ = JE* and *GK = KF*, so *K* and *J* are the midpoints of the legs of trapezoid *DEFG* by the definition of a midpoint. Since $\overline{JK}$ is the segment that connects the midpoints of the legs of a trapezoid, it is the median of the trapezoid based on the definition of a median. Since the median of a trapezoid is parallel to its bases, $\overline{JK}\|\overline{DG}$. When parallel lines are cut by a transversal, same-side interior angles are supplementary, so ∠*D* is supplementary to ∠*DJK*.

Practice *Write a paragraph proof.*

1. Given: $\overline{CG}\perp\overline{AE}$.
        I is the midpoint of $\overline{AE}$.
   Prove: △*AIC* ≅ △*EIC*.

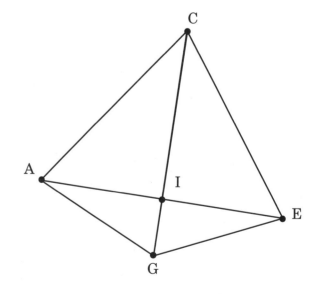

2. Given: △*JNO* is equiangular.

         LKOM is a parallelogram.

    Prove: △*JLK* is an equilateral triangle.

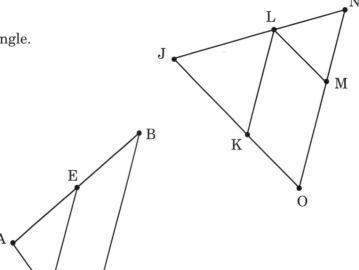

3. Given: △*ADE*~△*ACB*.

    Prove: $\overline{DE} \parallel \overline{BC}$.

4. Given: ∠*BAD* ≅ ∠*DBA* and $\overline{AC} \cong \overline{BC}$.

    Prove: ∠*DAC* ≅ ∠*CBD*.

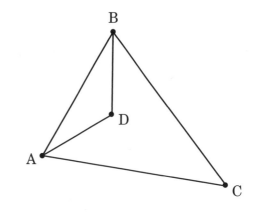

5. Given: $\overleftrightarrow{EI}$ and $\overleftrightarrow{DH}$ are tangent to ⊙*A*.

         ∠*EIG* is a right angle.

    Prove: *DEIH* is a rectangle.

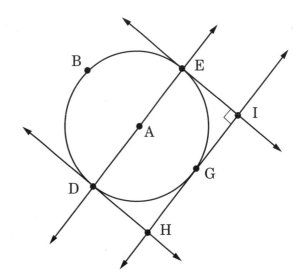

✓ Often there are at least two correct ways to write a proof.

Examples

Given: ∠*OQL* is supplementary to ∠*NRP.*
Prove: ∠*MQR* is supplementary to ∠*SRQ.*

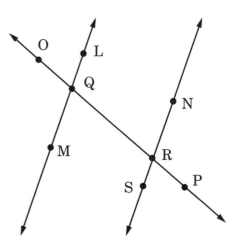

Approach A: Because vertical angles are congruent, it is possible to say that ∠*OQL* ≅ ∠*MQR* and ∠*NRP* ≅ ∠*SRQ*. According to the given, the first angle in each of these pairs makes a pair of supplementary angles. We are trying to prove that the second angle in each of these pairs forms a supplementary pair. Supplements of the same angle are congruent. That fact helps us through the following line of reasoning: Since

∠*NRP* is supplementary to ∠*OQL* and ∠*OQL* ≅ ∠*MQR*, ∠*NRP* is also a supplement of ∠*MQR*. Since ∠*MQR* is a supplement of ∠*NRP* and ∠*NRP* ≅ ∠*SRQ*, ∠*MQR* is a supplement of ∠*SRQ*.

Proof for Approach A: ∠*OQL* is supplementary to ∠*NRP*. ∠*OQL* ≅ ∠*MQR* because they are vertical angles. Since supplements of the same angle are congruent, ∠*NRP* must be a supplement of ∠*MQR*. ∠*NRP* ≅ ∠*SRQ* because they are vertical angles. Since supplements of the same angle are congruent, ∠*SRQ* must be supplementary to ∠*MQR*.

Approach B: In order to say that ∠*MQR* is supplementary to ∠*SRQ*, it would help to know that $\overleftrightarrow{LM} \parallel \overleftrightarrow{SN}$. We can prove that they are parallel if we know that a pair of corresponding angles are congruent. If we know that *m*∠*NRP* = *m*∠*LQR*, then we would have the pair of congruent corresponding angles we need.

Proof for Approach B: Since we are provided as Given that *m*∠*OQL* is supplementary to *m*∠*NRP*, we know that *m*∠*OQL* + *m*∠*NRP* = 180°. We also know, from the figure, that *m*∠*OQL* + *m*∠*LQR* = 180°, because two angles that form a straight angle equal the sum of 180°. By combining the two statements about supplementary angles, we can say that *m*∠*OQL* + *m*∠*NRP* = *m*∠*OQL* + *m*∠*LQR* by substitution. Using the subtraction property, we can subtract *m*∠*OQL* from both sides of the equation, getting *m*∠*NRP* = *m*∠*LQR*. Since the two angles are congruent and corresponding, we know that $\overleftrightarrow{LM} \parallel \overleftrightarrow{SN}$. We can now make the conclusion that ∠*MQR* and ∠*SRQ* are same-side interior angles, and are, therefore, supplementary.

Practice *Write 2 different paragraph proofs for each problem.*

1. Given: *X* and *U* are midpoints.
      ∠*YZU* and ∠*WVU* are right angles.
   Prove: *WVUX* is a trapezoid.

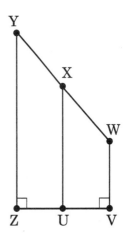

2. Given: $\overline{JK}$ and $\overline{LM}$ are parallel and congruent.
   Prove: △*JKN* ≅ △*MLN*.

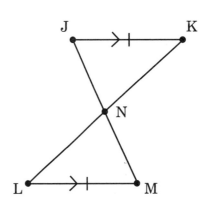

3. Given: *JHIK* is a square.
   Prove: △*JFH* ≅ △*KFI*.

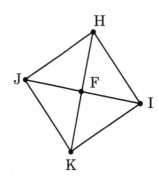

Chapter 6

Strategy #5

Strategy #5 Organize the facts into a logical argument.

✓ Now that you have practiced writing proofs in paragraph form, it is time to begin thinking about more formal proofs. To start, practice taking a list of steps and organizing them into a logical order for a convincing argument. As you put them in order, think about what reason you can give for each step. After you have put them in order, write the reasons which would justify each step in the order you have placed them.

For Example *Organize the facts into a logical argument, then supply the reasons for each step.*

Given: $\angle OLN \cong \angle PLM$
Prove: $\angle OLP \cong \angle NLM$

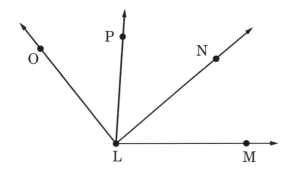

   4 $\angle OLP \cong \angle NLM$
   1 $\angle OLP + \angle PLN = \angle OLN$ and
          $\angle PLN + \angle NLM = \angle PLM$
   2 $\angle OLN \cong \angle PLM$
   3 $\angle OLP + \angle PLN = \angle PLN + \angle NLM$

Reasons:
1. Angle Addition
2. Given
3. Substitution
4. Subtraction

Practice *Organize the facts into a logical argument, then supply the reasons for each step.*

1. Given: $\overline{XZ} \cong \overline{QS}$ and $\overline{XY} \cong \overline{RS}$.
    Prove: $\overline{YZ} \cong \overline{QR}$.

    a. _____ $XY + YZ = QR + RS$
    b. _____ $\overline{XY} \cong \overline{RS}$
    c. _____ $\overline{XZ} \cong \overline{QS}$
    d. _____ $\overline{YZ} \cong \overline{QR}$
    e. _____ $XY + YZ = XZ$ and $QR + RS = QS$
    f. _____ $XY + YZ = QR + XY$

2. Given: $\overline{GH} \parallel \overline{IJ}$.
    Prove: $\triangle GKH \sim \triangle JKI$.

    a. _____ $\triangle GKH \sim \triangle JKI$
    b. _____ $\overline{GH} \parallel \overline{IJ}$
    c. _____ $\angle G \cong \angle J$ and $\angle H \cong \angle I$

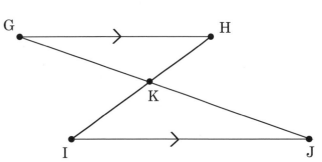

3. Given: $\overleftrightarrow{QR} \perp \overleftrightarrow{QP}$.

$\qquad m\angle TQR + m\angle SQP = 90°.$

Prove: $m\angle TQR = m\angle RQS.$

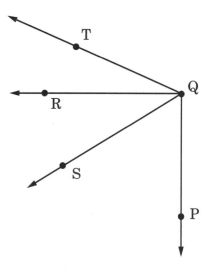

a. _____ $m\angle TQR + m\angle SQP = 90°$

b. _____ $m\angle RQP = 90°$

c. _____ $m\angle RQS + m\angle SQP = 90°$

d. _____ $m\angle TQR + m\angle SQP = m\angle RQS + m\angle SQP$

e. _____ $m\angle RQS + m\angle SQP = m\angle RQP$

f. _____ $\overleftrightarrow{QR} \perp \overleftrightarrow{QP}$

g. _____ $\angle RQP$ is a right angle.

h. _____ $m\angle TQR = m\angle RQS$

4. Given: $\overleftrightarrow{FG}$ is a tangent.

$\qquad B$ is a midpoint.

$\qquad BG = GF.$

Prove: $\triangle EFG$ is a 30–60–90 triangle.

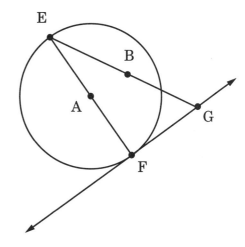

a. _____ $\triangle EFG$ is a right triangle.

b. _____ $BG = GF$

c. _____ $\cos m\angle BGF = \dfrac{GF}{EG}$

d. _____ $\angle BGF$ and $\angle BEA$ are complementary.

e. _____ $\triangle EFG$ is a 30–60–90 triangle.

f. _____ $\overleftrightarrow{FG}$ is a tangent.

g. _____ B is a midpoint.

h. _____ $BG = \frac{1}{2} EG$

i. _____ $GF = \frac{1}{2} EG$

j. _____ $\angle EFG$ is a right angle.

k. _____ $60° + m\angle BEA = 90°$

l. _____ $m\angle BGF = 60°$

m. _____ $\cos m\angle BGF = \dfrac{GF}{EG} = \dfrac{1}{2}$

n. _____ $m\angle BGF + m\angle BEA = 90°$

o. _____ $m\angle BEA = 30°$

p. _____ $\cos 60° = \frac{1}{2}$

q. _____ $\overline{EF} \perp \overleftrightarrow{FG}$

r. _____ $\dfrac{GF}{EG} = \dfrac{1}{2}$

5. Given: $\overline{IL}$ perpendicular bisector of $\overline{HK}$.
   Prove: $\angle JHL \cong \angle JKL$.

a. _____ $\triangle HIJ \cong \triangle KIJ$ and $\triangle HIL \cong \triangle KIL$
b. _____ $m\angle IHJ + m\angle JHL = m\angle IKJ + m\angle JKL$
c. _____ $\overline{IL}$ perpendicular bisector of $\overline{HK}$
d. _____ $\overline{IL} \cong \overline{IL}$ and $\overline{IJ} \cong \overline{IJ}$
e. _____ $\angle JHL \cong \angle JKL$
f. _____ $m\angle IHJ + m\angle JHL = m\angle IHL$
g. _____ $m\angle IKJ + m\angle JKL = m\angle IKL$
h. _____ $m\angle IHJ + m\angle JHL = m\angle IHJ + m\angle JKL$
i. _____ $\overline{HI} \cong \overline{IK}$
j. _____ $\angle HIL \cong \angle KIL$
k. _____ $\angle HIL$ and $\angle KIL$ are right angles.
l. _____ $\angle IHJ \cong \angle IKJ$
m. _____ $\angle IHL \cong \angle IKL$

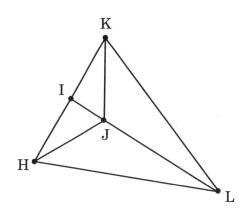

✓ Now you will practice the structure of a 2-column proof. On the left is a list of statements (facts) arranged in a logical order. On the right is the list of the reasons used to justify those statements. You should notice that the reasons and statements line up so that each reason explains how you got from the step before it to the current step.

For Example *Fill in the missing statements and reasons.*
   Given: $\triangle AEC$ and $\triangle DEB$ are isosceles triangles.
   Prove: $AB = CD$.

Statements	Reasons
1. $\triangle AEC$ and $\triangle DEB$ are isosceles triangles.	1.
2. $AE = EC$ and ____ = ____	2. Definition of an isosceles triangle
3. and	3. Segment Addition
4. $AE + EB = CD$ and $EC + ED = AB$	4.
5.	5. Substitution

Answers: Reasons
   2. $ED = EB$ 1. Given
   3. $AE + EB = AB$ and $EC + ED = CD$ 4. Subtitution
   5. $AB = CD$

Note: "Prove" is never a reason, it's part of the directions. Only postulates, theorems, definitions and properties can be reasons.

Practice *Fill in the missing statements and reasons.*

1. Given: ⊙*H*; points *I*, *J* and *K* are on the circle; *m* ∠*J* = 45°.
   Prove: △*IKJ* is an isosceles triangle.

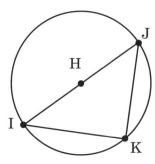

Statements	Reasons
1. ___	1. Given
2. $\overline{IJ}$ is a diameter.	2.
3.	3. Definition of semicircle
4.	4. If an angle is inscribed in a semicircle, then it is a right angle.
5. △*IJK* is a right triangle.	5.
6 ∠*I* and ∠*J* are complementary.	6.
7. ____ + ____ = ____	7. Definition of ____ ____
8. *m* ∠*J* = 45°	8.
9.	9. Substitution
10. *m* ∠*I* = 45°	10.
11.	11. If two angles of a triangle are congruent, then the sides opposite those angles are congruent.
12.	12.

2. Given: ∠*MQN* ≅ ∠*OTR*.
   Prove: $\overleftrightarrow{SN} \| \overrightarrow{OP}$.

Statements	Reasons
1. ∠*MQN* and ∠*NQT* are supplementary. ____ and ____ are supplementary.	1.
2.	2. Given
3. ∠*NQT* ≅ ∠*OTQ*	3.
4. $\overleftrightarrow{SN} \| \overrightarrow{OP}$	4.

3. Given: $\triangle BEC \cong \triangle DEA$.

Prove: E is the midpoint of $\overline{AC}$.

Statements	Reasons
1.	1.
2.	2. CPCTC
3. $\overline{CB} \parallel \overline{AD}$	3.
4.	4. CPCTC
5. $ABCD$ is a parallelogram.	5. If one pair of opposite sides of a quadrilateral are both congruent and parallel, then the quadrilateral is a parallelogram.
6.	6. The diagonals of a parallelogram bisect each other.
7.	7.

4. Given: $\triangle PQR \cong \triangle TSR$.

Prove: $\triangle PQS \cong \triangle TSQ$.

Statements	Reasons
1. $\triangle PQR \cong \triangle TSR$	1.
2. $\angle P \cong \angle T$; $\angle PQR \cong \angle TSR$; $\overline{QR} \cong \overline{RS}$; $\overline{PQ} \cong \overline{TS}$	2.
3.	3. Definition of isosceles triangle
4. $\angle RQS \cong \angle RSQ$	4.
5. $\angle PQR + \angle RQS \cong \angle TSR + \angle RSQ$	5.
6. and	6. Angle addition
7. $\angle PQS \cong \angle TSQ$	7.
8.	8. ASA

5. Given: trapezoid $UVXY$; W and Z are midpoints.

Prove: $WZUV$ is a trapezoid.

Statements	Reasons
1.	1.
2.	2. Definition of median
3. $\overline{WZ} \parallel \overline{VU}$	3.
4.	4.

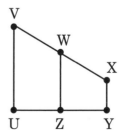

Chapter 7

Strategy #6

Formal Proofs

Strategy #6: Write formal proofs in 2-column form.

✓ In the second half of Strategy 5 you were introduced to the 2-column proof. This is a formal, organizational tool for proof-writing. It allows you to make statements in one column and justifications (reasons) in the second column. By lining up the statements with the reasons which defend them, it is easy for anyone to read your proof and understand what you are saying.

✓ The strategies in this workbook have been designed to help you develop the skills and thinking patterns you need to write formal proofs. As you work on proofs, think back to the exercises in this workbook. If you are stuck in a proof, use the methods of the workbook to help you:

• Stop thinking about what you're trying to prove and try brainstorming about the figure itself.

• Work backwards from what you are trying to prove. Ask yourself, "What would I need to know to state this?"

• Write steps for different parts of the proof and then try to fit them together.

• Allow yourself to make mistakes, run into 'dead ends' with lines of reasoning; eventually you'll find a line of reasoning that leads to what you are trying to prove.

• Sometimes writing a paragraph proof first can lay out the thinking before switching over to a formal 2-column proof (sometimes the 2-column proof is easier and the paragraph proof comes later…it depends on the proof and the person).

For Example *Write a proof in 2-column form.*
Given: $\angle 1 \cong \angle 2$.
Prove: $\overline{AB} \| \overline{CD}$.

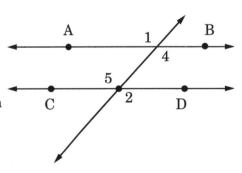

Think about the problem before you try to write the proof:
$\angle 1$ and $\angle 2$ don't have a direct relationship. However, they both have vertical angles which are shown in the figure. $\angle 1$ and $\angle 4$ form a pair of vertical angles, and $\angle 2$ and $\angle 5$ form a pair of vertical angles. Since we know that pairs of vertical angles are congruent, we can use that relationship, combined with the transitive property, to show that $\angle 4$ and $\angle 5$ are congruent. Since $\angle 4$ and $\angle 5$ are alternate interior angles and since we will be able to show that they are congruent, we will be able to conclude that these lines are parallel.

Statements	Reasons
1. $\angle 1 \cong \angle 2$	1. Given
2. $\angle 1 \cong \angle 4$; $\angle 5 \cong \angle 2$	2. Vertical angles are congruent.
3. $\angle 4 \cong \angle 5$	3. Substitution
4. $\overline{AB} \| \overline{CD}$	4. Alternate interior angles

Practice *Write a proof in 2-column form.*

1. Given: △*ACE* and △*AGE* are isosceles
    triangles with $\overline{AE}$ as their base.
    Prove: Quadrilateral *ACEG* is a kite.

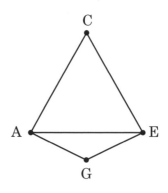

2. Given: $\overline{AD} \| \overline{BC}$; ∠*DAB* ≅ ∠*EAC*.
    Prove: △*ABC* is an isosceles triangle.

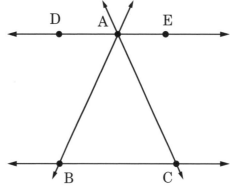

3. Given: *V* and *W* are midpoints; *RU = RV*.
    Prove: *RS = 2RU*.

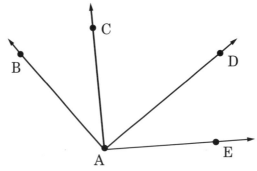

4. Given: ∠*BAC* ≅ ∠*EAD*.
    Prove: ∠*BAD* ≅ ∠*CAE*.

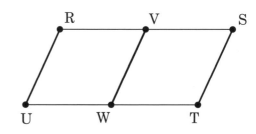

5. Given: ∠*BAD* and ∠*ADC* are right angles.
    Prove: *EABC* is a trapezoid.

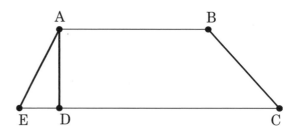

✓ Some proofs are really 2 or 3 smaller proofs combined. In other words, the given statements are not directly connected to what is to be proved. Instead you have to prove some other facts about the picture first, and then use those facts to get to what it is that you are supposed to prove. This requires some higher order thinking. It might also mean that you try a few different approaches before you find the one (or ones) that lead to what you really have to prove.

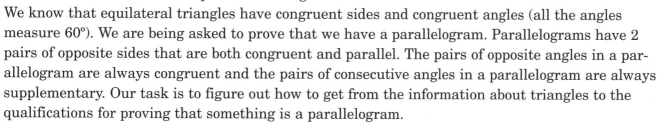

For Example *Write a proof in 2-column form.*

Given: △*ABC*, △*BDE* and △*EFC* are equilateral triangles.
Prove: quadrilateral *ADEF* is a parallelogram.

Think about what you are trying to do before you jump into the structure of the 2-column proof.

✓ We are told that we have equilateral triangles.
We know that equilateral triangles have congruent sides and congruent angles (all the angles measure 60°). We are being asked to prove that we have a parallelogram. Parallelograms have 2 pairs of opposite sides that are both congruent and parallel. The pairs of opposite angles in a parallelogram are always congruent and the pairs of consecutive angles in a parallelogram are always supplementary. Our task is to figure out how to get from the information about triangles to the qualifications for proving that something is a parallelogram.

✓ Start by drawing in all of the angles that you know to be congruent (and to have a measure of 60°) based on the fact that we have 3 equilateral triangles: ∠*B*, ∠*C*, ∠*A*, ∠*BDE*, ∠*DEB*, ∠*CFE* and ∠*FEC*. When you do this you should notice that ∠*DEB* and ∠*FEC* are both 60° and that the angle in between them, ∠*DEF*, completes a straight angle; *m* ∠*DEB* + *m* ∠*DEF* *m* ∠*FEC* = 180°, so 60° + *m* ∠*DEF* + 60° = 180° and that means that *m* ∠*DEF* = 60° as well. Therefore you can also draw congruent marks on your picture for ∠*DEF*.

✓ Looking at your picture, you should notice that ∠*A* and ∠*DEF* are a pair of opposite angles which we have just shown to be congruent. If we could also show that the other pair of opposite angles were congruent, we'd be able to show that this is a parallelogram. Well, we already know that ∠*BDE* and ∠*EFC* are 60°. Each of those angles forms a straight angle with ∠*ADE* and ∠*AFE,* respectively. Since pairs of adjacent angles which form a straight angle are supplementary, and since supplements of congruent angles are congruent, ∠*ADE* must be congruent to ∠*AFE*, though they are not congruent to all of the 60° angles in the picture (rather, their measure is 120°). That gives us a quadrilateral in which both pairs of opposite angles are congruent, so it is a parallelogram. Now it's time to write these thoughts in the form of a 2-column proof.

Statements	Reasons
1. △ABC, △BDE and △EFC are equilateral triangles.	1. Given
2. △ABC, △BDE and △EFC are equiangular triangles.	2. All equilateral triangles are also equiangular.
3. $m\angle A = 60°$; $m\angle B = 60°$; $m\angle C = 60°$; $m\angle BDE = 60°$; $m\angle DEB = 60°$; $m\angle CFE = 60°$; $m\angle FEC = 60°$	3. The measure of one angle in an equiangular triangle is 60°.
4. $m\angle A = m\angle B = m\angle C = m\angle BDE$ $= m\angle DEB = m\angle CFE = m\angle FEC$	4. Substitution
5. $m\angle BED + m\angle DEF + m\angle FEC = 180°$	5. Angle addition/straight angle
6. $60° + m\angle DEF + 60° = 180°$	6. Substitution
7. $m\angle DEF = 60°$	7. Subtraction
8. $m\angle DEF = m\angle A$	8. Substitution
9. $m\angle BDE + m\angle ADE = 180°$; $m\angle AFE + m\angle EFC = 180°$	9. Angle addition/straight angle
10. $60° + m\angle ADE = 180°$; $60° + m\angle EFC = 180°$	10. Substitution
11. $m\angle ADE = 120°$; $m\angle EFA = 120°$	11. Subtraction
12. $m\angle ADE = m\angle EFA$	12. Substitution
13. Quadrilateral ADEF is a parallelogram.	13. If both pairs of opposite angles of a quadrilateral are congruent, then the quadrilateral is a parallelogram.

Practice *Write a proof in 2-column form.*

1. Given: $\overline{LM} \cong \overline{MJ}$ and $\overline{LI} \cong \overline{IK}$.
   Prove: $m\angle MIK + m\angle JKI = 180°$.

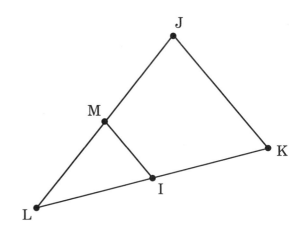

2. Given: $\angle JAK \cong \angle ADL \cong \angle GBA$.
Prove: *ABED* is a parallelogram.

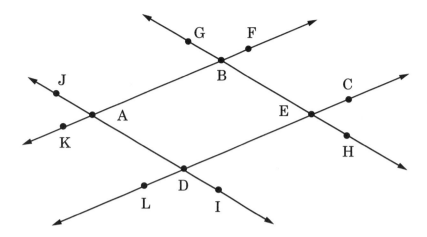

3. Given: *I* and *F* are midpoints on parallelogram *EGJH*.
$\overline{IF} \cong \overline{IG}$; $\overline{FJ} \cong \overline{GJ}$.
Prove: *EIFH* is a rhombus.

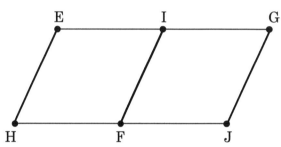

4. Given: $\triangle WXY \cong \triangle YZW$; $XY^2 + XW^2 = WY^2$.
Prove: *WXYZ* is a rectangle.

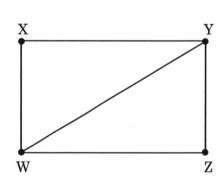

5. Given: *GIJF* is a trapezoid.
$m \angle HJI + m \angle HIJ = m \angle F$.
Prove: *FGHJ* is a parallelogram.

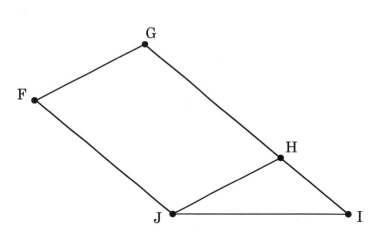

Sometimes there are multiple ways to prove the same conclusion. Practicing multiple proofs for the same problem helps you to develop your creativity in proof-writing.

Practice *Write at least 2 distinct proofs for each problem. This means that you will write two proofs for #1 and 2 proofs for #2. Remember that the proofs need to be different from each other. Try to imagine the problem from a totally different perspective.*

1. Given: *STUV* is a parallelogram.
   Prove: Δ*VSU* ≅ Δ*TUS*.

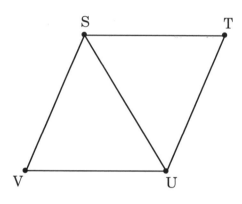

2. Given: ∠*I* ≅ ∠*E*; *O* is a midpoint; ∠*AOE* is a right angle.
   Prove: ∠*IAO* ≅ ∠*EAO*.

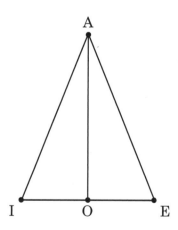

Explore the Possibilities

In this section, use the same picture but different sets of given information and write at least 4 different proofs for each figure. Note: Answers for this section are not included in the answer key because there are innumerable potential responses.

Write a series of proofs all about this one figure.

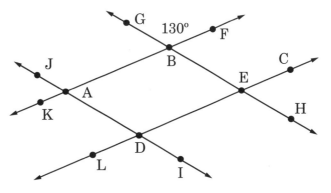

Write a series of proofs all about this one figure.

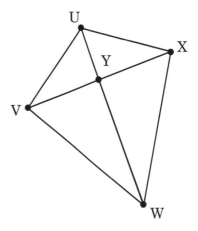

Write a series of proofs all about this one figure.
Given: ΔVUS is equilateral and RQTS is a parallelogram.

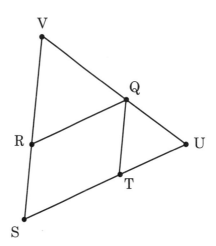

Glossary

Algebra

Addition: If $a = b$, then $a + c = b + c$. Also, if $a = b$ and $c = d$, then $a + c = b + d$.

Reflexive Property: $a = a$.

Substitution Property: If $a = b$, then a can be used in place of b in any situation.

Transitive Property: If $a = b$ and $b = c$, then $a = c$.

Angles

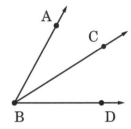

An acute angle has a measure less than 90°.

An obtuse angle has a measure greater than 90°, but less than 180°.

Angle Addition: $m \angle ABC + m \angle CBD = m \angle ABD$.

Bisector

Definition: A ray which divides an angle into two congruent parts.

Angle Bisector Theorem: If $\overrightarrow{BC}$ is an angle bisector, then
$m \angle ABC = m \angle CBD = \frac{1}{2} m \angle ABD$.

Segment Bisector: a plane, point, line, ray or segment which divides a segment into two congruent parts. One of the segments formed by a segment bisector is equal in length to half the length of the original segment.

Circle

Definition: A collection of points equidistant from a single point.

A radius is a segment which connects the center of a circle with a point on the circle.

All radii in a circle are congruent.

A diameter is a chord which passes through the center of a circle.

The length of a diameter is twice the length of a radius.

A line which intersects the circle in exactly one point (the point of tangency) is called a tangent line.

A tangent is perpendicular to the radius which intersects it at the point of tangency.

A semicircle is an arc whose endpoints are the endpoints of a diameter.

If an angle is inscribed in a semicircle, then it is a right angle.

Complementary Angles

Definition: Two angles whose sum is 90°.

If two adjacent angles form a right angle, then they are complementary.

If two angles are complements of the same angle, or of congruent angles, then they are congruent. (Complements of congruent angles are congruent.)

The acute angles of a right triangle are complementary.

Congruent Triangles

Definition: Triangles with congruent corresponding sides and congruent corresponding angles.

SSS: If the sides of one triangle are congruent to the corresponding sides of another triangle, then the triangles are congruent.

SAS: If two sides and the included angle of one triangle are congruent to the corresponding parts of another triangle, then the triangles are congruent.

ASA: If two angles and the included side of one triangle are congruent to the corresponding parts of another triangle, then the triangles are congruent.

AAS: If two angles and a non-included side of one triangle are congruent to the corresponding parts of another triangle, then the triangles are congruent.

HL: If the hypotenuse and leg of one triangle are congruent to the corresponding parts of another right triangle, then the triangles are congruent.

CPCTC: Corresponding parts of congruent triangles are congruent.

Equiangular Polygon

Definition: A polygon in which all angles are congruent.

All equiangular triangles are also equilateral.

The measure of one angle in an equiangular triangle is 60°.

Equilateral Polygon

Definition: A polygon in which all sides are congruent.

All equilateral triangles are also equiangular.

Equiangular Triangle

Definition: A triangle in which all angles are congruent.

Equilateral Triangle

Definition: A triangle in which all sides are congruent.

Isosceles Trapezoid

Definition: A trapezoid with congruent legs.

There are two pairs of congruent base angles.

The diagonals are congruent.

Isosceles Triangle

Definition: A triangle with at least 2 congruent sides.

The base angles are congruent.

The altitude from the vertex angle of an isosceles triangle is also a median, a perpendicular bisector and an angle bisector.

If two angles of a triangle are congruent, then the sides opposite those angles are congruent.

Kite

Definition: A quadrilateral with two pairs of congruent adjacent sides.

The diagonals are perpendicular.

Parallel Lines

Definition: Coplanar lines which do not intersect.

Same-side interior angles are supplementary.

Alternate interior angles are congruent.

Corresponding angles are congruent.

If two lines are perpendicular to the same line, then they are parallel.

Parallelogram

Definition: A quadrilateral with two pairs of parallel sides.

Both pairs of opposite sides of a parallelogram are congruent.

Both pairs of opposite angles of a parallelogram are congruent.

Consecutive angles of a parallelogram are congruent.

The diagonals of a parallelogram bisect each other.

Polygon

Definition: A figure with at least 3 sides. The sides of a polygon are segments. None of the sides intersect each other, except at the vertices of the polygon.

The number of degrees in a convex polygon is $(n-2)180°$, where n is the number of sides.

The sum of the exterior angles of any convex polygon is $360°$.

Rectangle

Definition: A parallelogram with 4 right angles. An equiangular parallelogram.

The diagonals of a rectangle are congruent.

A rectangle has 4 right angles.

Regular Polygon

Definition: A polygon which is equilateral and equiangular.

The measure of an interior angle in a regular polygon is $\frac{(n-2)180}{n}$, where n is the number of sides.

Rhombus

Definition: A parallelogram with 4 congruent sides or a quadrilateral with four congruent sides. An equilateral parallelogram.

The diagonals of a rhombus bisect the angles.

The diagonals of a rhombus are perpendicular.

Right Angle

Definition: An angle with a measure of 90°.

Perpendicular lines intersect to form right angles.

Right Triangle

Definition: A triangle with one right angle.

Pythagorean Theorem: In a right triangle, the square of the hypotenuse is equal to the sum of the squares of the legs.

The acute angles of a right triangle are complementary.

The altitude to the hypotenuse divides the triangle into two triangles which are similar to the original right triangle.

The median to the hypotenuse is equal in length to half of the hypotenuse.

Segment

Segment Addition: If A is a point on $\overline{BC}$, then $BA + AC = BC$.

Similar Triangles

Definition: Triangles with congruent corresponding angles and corresponding sides which are in proportion.

SAS: If two sides of one triangle are proportional to two sides of another triangle and the included angles are congruent, then the triangles are similar.

SSS: If the sides of one triangle are in proportion to the sides of another triangle, then the triangles are similar.

AA: If two angles of one triangle are congruent to two angles of another triangle, then the triangles are similar.

Congruent triangles are similar.

Square

Definition: A regular parallelogram.

A square is a rhombus.

A square is a rectangle.

Supplementary Angles

Definition: Two angles whose sum is 180°.

If two adjacent angles form a line, they are supplementary.

If two angles are supplements of the same angle, or of congruent angles, then they are congruent. (Supplements of congruent angles are congruent.)

Trapezoids

Definition: A quadrilateral with exactly one pair of parallel sides.

Definition: The median of a trapezoid is the segment which connects the midpoints of the legs.

The median of a trapezoid is parallel to the bases and is half as long as the sum of the lengths of the bases.

Triangle

Definition: A 3-sided polygon.

The sum of the interior angles of a triangle is 180°.

The measure of an exterior angle of a triangle is equal to the sum of the remote interior angles.

Midpoint Connector: The segment which connects the midpoints of 2 sides of a triangle is parallel to the third side of the triangle and has a length which is half the length of the third side. (Note: Different textbooks use different words to name this term. Some call it a midsegment; others don't give it a name.)

An altitude of a triangle is a segment from a vertex to the opposite side which is perpendicular to that side.

Vertical Angles

Definition: Two nonadjacent angles formed when two lines intersect.

Vertical angles are congruent.

Answer Key

Note: This answer key is a thorough treatment of each problem. However, there may be additional correct answers which do not appear in this answer key. If in doubt, check your work against the explanations in this workbook or your own textbook. If you are still unsure, check with a teacher or classmate.

Pages 6–7

1. *UMIO* is a rhombus; given. *UMIO* is a parallelogram with four congruent sides, so $UM = MI = IO = OU$; definition of a rhombus. $\overleftrightarrow{UM} \parallel \overleftrightarrow{OI}$ and $\overleftrightarrow{UO} \parallel \overleftrightarrow{MI}$; definition of a parallelogram. $\angle U \cong \angle I$ and $\angle O \cong \angle M$; opposite angles of a parallelogram are congruent. $\angle O$ and $\angle U$, $\angle U$ and $\angle M$, $\angle M$ and $\angle I$, and $\angle I$ and $\angle O$ are pairs of supplementary angles; when parallel lines are cut by a transversal, same side interior angles are supplementary.

2. $\triangle WYL$ is an isosceles triangle; given. $\overline{WY} \cong \overline{YL}$; the legs of an isosceles triangle are congruent. $m \angle W + m \angle L + m \angle Y = 180°$; the sum of the measures of the interior angles of a triangle is 180°. $\angle Y \cong \angle L$; the base angles of an isosceles triangle are congruent. $m \angle W = 36°$; given in the picture. $180° - 36° = 144° = m \angle L + m \angle W$; subtraction. Since $m \angle L = m \angle W$, each angle has a measure of $\frac{144°}{2} = 72°$.

3. $\overleftrightarrow{XH} \parallel \overleftrightarrow{EQ}$; given. $\overleftrightarrow{ZF}$ is a transversal; definition of a transversal. $\angle ZGX \cong \angle GVE$ and $\angle XGV \cong \angle EVF$ and $\angle ZGH \cong \angle GVQ$ and $\angle HGV \cong \angle QVF$; corresponding angles are congruent when parallel lines are cut by a transversal. $\angle ZGX \cong \angle HGV$ and $\angle ZGH \cong \angle XGV$ and $\angle GVE \cong \angle QVF$ and $\angle GVQ \cong \angle EVF$ vertical angles are congruent. $\angle XGV \cong \angle GVQ$ and $\angle HGV \cong \angle GVE$; alternate interior angles are congruent when parallel lines are cut by a transversal. $\angle HGV$ and $\angle QVG$ are supplementary angles, $\angle XGV$ and $\angle EVG$ are supplementary angles; same-side interior angles are supplementary when parallel lines are cut by a transversal. $\angle ZGX \cong \angle HGV \cong \angle GVE \cong \angle QVF$; substitution. $\angle ZGH \cong \angle XGV \cong \angle GVQ \cong \angle EVF$; substitution.

4. $\angle NPA$ is a right angle; given. $\angle APD$ and $\angle DPN$ are complementary angles; if two adjacent angles form a right angle, then they are complementary. $\angle APD$ and $\angle NPD$ are acute angles; definition of acute angles. $m \angle APN = 90°$; definition of a right angle. $m \angle APD + m \angle DPN = m \angle APN$ angle addition.

5. $\overrightarrow{BJ}$ is an angle bisector; given. $\angle RBJ \cong \angle JBW$; definition of an angle bisector. $m \angle RBJ = \frac{1}{2} \angle RBW = m \angle JBW$; angle bisector theorem. $m \angle RBJ + m \angle JBW = m \angle RBW$; angle addition.

6. *OBIQPD* is a hexagon; given. *OBIQPD* has six sides; definition of a hexagon. The sum of the measures of the interior angles of *OBIQPD* is $(6 - 2)180° = 720°$; the sum of the

45

measures of the interior angles of a complex polygon is $(n - 2)180°$. This appears to be an irregular polygon.

7. *TYGH* is a square; given. *TYGH* is a parallelogram with four congruent sides and four right angles; definition of a square. *TY = YG = HG = TH*; definition of a square. $m \angle T = m \angle Y = m \angle G = m \angle H = 90°$; definition of a regular polygon and $\frac{(n-2)\,180}{n}$ where n is the number of sides in a regular polygon. $\angle T, \angle Y, \angle H, \angle G$ are all right angles; definition of a right angle. *TYGH* is a quadrilateral; definition of a square. The sum of the measures of all of the interior angles is $(4 - 2)180° = 360°$; the sum of the measures of the interior angles of a convex polygon is $(n - 2)180°$.

8. $\overline{SF}$ is an altitude; given. $\angle ASL$ is a right angle; given from the picture. $\triangle SAL$ is a right triangle; definition of a right triangle. $\overline{SF}$ is perpendicular to $\overline{AL}$; definition of an altitude. $\angle AFS$ and $\angle SFL$ are right angles; definition of perpendicular lines. $\overline{AL}$ is the hypotenuse of $\triangle ASL$; definition of a hypotenuse. $\triangle AFS$ and $\triangle SFL$ are right triangles; definition of a right triangle. $\triangle AFS \sim \triangle SFL \sim \triangle ASL$; when the altitude is drawn to the hypotenuse of a right triangle, it forms two right triangles which are similar to each other and to the original triangle. $\angle A$ and $\angle L$ are complementary, $\angle A$ and $\angle ASF$ are complementary, $\angle L$ and $\angle FSL$ are complementary; the acute angles of a right triangle are complementary. $\angle A \cong \angle FSL$ and $\angle L \cong \angle ASF$; complements of the same angle are congruent. $\angle A \cong \angle FSL$ and $\angle L \cong \angle ASF$; corresponding angles in similar triangles are congruent by definition of similar triangles.

Pages 8–9

1. $\overline{AB} \cong \overline{EF}$ and $\overline{AG} \cong \overline{HF}$; given. $AG + GB = AB$ and $EH + HF = EF$; segment addition. $AG + GB = AB = EF = EH + HF$; substitution. $HF + GB = AB$ or $AG + EH = EF$; substitution. $AG + GB = EF$ and $HF + GB = EF$ but $HF + EH = EF$, so by subtraction $EH = GB$ (they're in the same position in the two equations and everything else in the two equations is the same).

2. $\overrightarrow{QR} \perp \overrightarrow{QP}$ and $m \angle TQR + m \angle SQP = 90°$; given. $\angle RQP$ is a right angle; definition of perpendicular rays. $m \angle RQP = 90°$; definition of right angles. $m \angle SQP + m \angle SQR = m \angle RQP$; angle addition. $m \angle SQP + m \angle SQR = m \angle RQP$, so $m \angle SQP + m \angle SQR = 90°$; substitution. $m \angle SQP + m \angle SQR = m \angle TQR + m \angle SQP$; substitution (they both equal 90°). $m \angle SQR = m \angle TQR$; subtraction (subtract $m \angle SQP$ from both sides of the previous equation). $\angle PQS$ and $\angle SQR$ are complementary, $\angle TQR$ and $\angle SPQ$ are complementary; definition of complementary angles.

3. $\overline{CG} \perp \overline{AE}$ and I is the midpoint of $\overline{AE}$; given. $\angle CIA, \angle AIG, \angle GIE, \angle EIC$ are right angles; definition of perpendicular lines. $AI = IE$; definition of a midpoint. $\triangle AIG \cong \triangle EIG$ and $\triangle AIC \cong \triangle EIC$; SAS (the congruent sides, the right angles, a shared side). $\angle GAE \cong \angle GEI, \angle AGI \cong \angle EGI, AG = GE$ and $\angle CAI \cong \angle CEI, \angle ACI \cong \angle ECI, AC = CE$; CPCTC. *AGEC* is a kite; definition of a kite.

4. $\triangle JNO$ is equiangular and $LKOM$ is a parallelogram; given. $\triangle JNO$ is equilateral; all equiangular triangles are equilateral. $m \angle J = m \angle N = m \angle O = 60°$; the measures of the angles of an equilateral triangle are 60°. $\overline{LK} \| \overline{OM}$ and $\overline{KO} \| \overline{LM}$; definition of a parallelogram. $\overline{LM} \cong \overline{KO}$ and $\overline{LK} \cong \overline{MO}$; opposite sides of a parallelogram are congruent. $\angle LKO \cong \angle LMO$ and $\angle KLM \cong \angle O$; opposite angles of a parallelogram are congruent. $m \angle MLK = 60°$; substitution. $m \angle NML = m \angle O = 60°$ and $m \angle JKL = m \angle O = 60°$; when parallel lines are cut by a transversal, corresponding angles are congruent. $m \angle NML + m \angle N + m \angle NLM = 180°$; the sum of the interior angles of a triangle is 180°. $60° + 60° + m \angle NLM = 180°$; substitution. $m \angle NLM = 60°$; subtraction. $\triangle LNM$ is equiangular; definition of an equiangular triangle. $\triangle LNM$ is equilateral, all equiangular triangles are equilateral. $m \angle JLK + m \angle KLM + m \angle MLN = m \angle JLN$; angle addition. $m \angle JLK + m \angle KLM + m \angle MLN = m \angle JLN = 180°$; the measure of a straight angle is 180°. $m \angle JLK + 60° + 60° = 180°$; substitution. $m \angle JLK = 60°$. $\triangle JKL$ is an equiangular triangle; definition of an equiangular triangle. $\triangle JKL$ is equilateral, all equiangular triangles are equilateral. $JK = KL = JL = MO$ and $LM = MN = LN = KO$ and $JN = NO = OJ$; the sides of an equilateral triangle are congruent and opposite sides of a parallelogram are congruent. $m \angle LKO = m \angle LMO = 120°$; you can determine that because same-side interior angles are supplementary or based on two angles which form a straight angle are supplementary.

5. $\angle BAD \cong \angle DBA$ and $\overline{AC} \cong \overline{BC}$; given. $\overline{BD} \cong \overline{DA}$; if two angles of a triangle are congruent, then the sides opposite those angles are congruent. $\triangle BDA$ is an isosceles triangle and $\triangle ABC$ is an isosceles triangle; definition of an isosceles triangle. $\angle BAC \cong \angle CBA$; base angles of an isosceles triangle are congruent. $m \angle BAC = m \angle BAD + m \angle DAC$ and $m \angle CBA = m \angle ABD + m \angle DBC$; angle addition. $m \angle CBA = m \angle BAD + m \angle DAC$; substitution. $m \angle CBA = m \angle ABD + m \angle DAC$; substitution. $\angle DBC \cong \angle DAC$; subtraction.

6. $RTSU$ is a parallelogram and $m \angle RTS = 53°$; given. $\overline{RT} \| \overline{US}$ and $\overline{RU} \| \overline{ST}$; definition of a parallelogram. $\overline{RT} \cong \overline{US}$ and $\overline{RU} \cong \overline{ST}$; opposite sides of a parallelogram are congruent. $\angle U \cong \angle T$ and $\angle URT \cong \angle UST$; opposite angles of a parallelogram are congruent. $m \angle U = m \angle T = 53°$; substitution. $\angle U$ and $\angle URT$ are supplementary and $\angle T$ and $\angle TSU$ are supplementary; same-side interior angles are supplementary when parallel lines are cut by a transversal. $m \angle U + m \angle URT = 180°$ and $m \angle T + m \angle TSU = 180°$; definition of supplementary angles. $53° + m \angle URT = 180°$ and $53° + m \angle TSU = 180°$; substitution. $m \angle URT = 127°$ and $m \angle TSU = 127°$; subtraction. $\angle URT \cong \angle TSU$; definition of congruent angles. $\angle URS \cong \angle TSR$ and $\angle TRS \cong \angle RSU$; alternate interior angles are congruent when parallel lines are cut by a transversal. $\triangle URS \cong \triangle TSR$; AAS (using the shared side) or ASA (using the shared side) or SSS or SAS.

Page 12

1. *line 1:* $\overleftrightarrow{AB}\|\overleftrightarrow{CD}$; given.

   $\angle EAB \cong \angle ACD$; corresponding angles.

   $m\angle ACD = 55°$; given.

   $m\angle EAB = 55°$; substitution.

   line 2: $\overleftrightarrow{AB}\|\overleftrightarrow{CD}$; given.

   $\angle ACD$ and $\angle BAC$ are supplementary; same-side interior angles.

   $m\angle ACD + m\angle BAC = 180°$; definition of supplementary angles.

   $m\angle ACD = 55°$; given.

   $55° + m\angle BAC = 180°$; substitution.

   $m\angle BAC = 125°$; subtraction.

   line 3: $\overleftrightarrow{BD}\perp\overleftrightarrow{CD}$. $\overleftrightarrow{AB}\|\overleftrightarrow{CD}$; given.

   $\overleftrightarrow{AB}\perp\overleftrightarrow{BD}$; if a line is perpendicular to one of a pair of parallel lines, then it is perpendicular to the other in the pair as well.

   $\angle ABD$ and $\angle CDB$ are right angles; definition of perpendicular lines.

   line 4: $\overleftrightarrow{AB}\|\overleftrightarrow{CD}$; given.

   $ABDC$ is a trapezoid; definition of a trapezoid ($\overline{AB}$ and $\overline{CD}$ are bases of this trapezoid).

2. *line 1:* G and I are midpoints; given.

   $FG = GH$ and $FI = IJ$; definition of a midpoint.

   line 2: G and I are midpoints; given.

   $FG = \frac{1}{2}FH$, $GH = \frac{1}{2}FH$, $FI = \frac{1}{2}FJ$ and $IJ = \frac{1}{2}FJ$; midpoint theorem.

   line 3: G and I are midpoints; given.

   $\overline{GI}\|\overline{HJ}$; if a segment connects the midpoints of two sides of a triangle, it is parallel to the third side.

   $\angle FGI \cong \angle FHJ$ and $\angle FIG \cong \angle FJH$; corresponding angles are congruent.

   $\Delta FHJ \sim \Delta FGI$; AA~.

   line 4: G and I are midpoints; given.

   $GI = \frac{1}{2}HJ$; if a segment connects the midpoints of two sides of a triangle, it is half as long as the third side.

   $FG = \frac{1}{2}FH$, $FI = \frac{1}{2}FJ$; midpoint theorem.

   $\Delta FGI \sim \Delta FHJ$; the sides are in proportion, definition of similar triangles or SSS~.

3. *line 1:* $MNOP$ and $PQRS$ are parallelograms; given.

   $\overline{PS}\|\overline{QR}$, $\overline{PO}\|\overline{MN}$, $\overline{PM}\|\overline{ON}$, $\overline{PQ}\|\overline{SR}$; definition of a parallelogram.

$\overline{QR}\|\overline{MN}$ and $\overline{ON}\|\overline{SR}$; if two lines are parallel to the same line then they are parallel to each other.

line 2: MNOP and *PQRS* are parallelograms; given.

$\overline{PM}\cong\overline{ON}$, $\overline{PO}\cong\overline{MN}$, $\overline{SP}\cong\overline{RQ}$, $\overline{SR}\cong\overline{RQ}$; opposite sides of a parallelogram are congruent.

line 3: MNOP and *PQRS* are parallelograms; given.

$\angle S\cong\angle Q$, $\angle P\cong\angle R$, $\angle P\cong\angle N$, $\angle PON\cong\angle PMN$; opposite angles in a parallelogram are congruent, $\angle N\cong\angle R$; transitive property.

line 4: MNOP and *PQRS* are parallelograms; given.

$\overline{PS}\|\overline{QR}$, $\overline{PO}\|\overline{MN}$, $\overline{PM}\|\overline{ON}$, $\overline{PQ}\|\overline{SR}$; definition of a parallelogram.

$\angle PON\cong\angle S$, $\angle PMN\cong\angle Q$; corresponding angles are congruent.

4. *line 1*: *VZXY* is a rhombus.

$\overline{VX}\perp\overline{YZ}$; the diagonals of a rhombus are perpendicular.

$\angle VWY$, $\angle XWY$, $\angle VWZ$ and $\angle XWZ$ are right angles; definition of perpendicular lines. $\triangle VWY$, $\triangle XWY$, $\triangle VWZ$ and $\triangle XWZ$ are right triangles; definition of right triangle.

line 2: *VZXY* is a rhombus.

$VZ = ZX = XY = YV$; definition of a rhombus.

line 3: *VZXY* is a rhombus.

VZXY is a parallelogram: definition of a rhombus.

$\overline{VZ}\|\overline{YX}$ and $\overline{VY}\|\overline{ZX}$; definition of a parallelogram.

$\angle ZVX\cong\angle YXV$, $\angle YVX\cong\angle VXZ$, $\angle VZY\cong\angle XYZ$, $\angle VYZ\cong\angle XZY$; alternate interior angles are congruent.

line 4: *VZXY* is a rhombus.

$\overline{VY}\cong\overline{VZ}\cong\overline{ZX}\cong\overline{XY}$; definiton of a rhombus.

VZXY is a parallelogram; definition of a rhombus.

$\overline{VX}$ and $\overline{YZ}$ bisect each other; the diagonals of a parallelogram bisect each other.

$\overline{VW}\cong\overline{WX}$ and $\overline{YW}\cong\overline{WZ}$; definition of a segment bisector.

$\triangle VWY\cong\triangle XWY\cong\triangle XWZ\cong\triangle VWZ$; SSS.

5. *line 1*: $\triangle IWR$ and $\triangle WYI$ are right triangles; given.

$\angle WYI$ is a right angle; definition of a right triangle.

$\angle WYR$ is a right angle; if two adjacent angles form a straight angle and one of the angles is a right angle, then the other angle is also a right angle.

$\overline{WY}\perp\overline{IR}$; definition of perpendicular lines.

$\overline{WY}$ is an altitude; definition of an altitude.

$\triangle WYI \sim \triangle RYW \sim \triangle RWI$; the altitude to the hypotenuse of a right triangle forms two right triangles which are similar to each other and to the original triangle.

$\angle WIY \cong \angle YWR$ and $\angle WRY \cong \angle IWY$; corresponding angles in similar triangles are congruent.

line 2: $\triangle IWR$ is a right triangle; given.

$\angle I$ and $\angle R$ are complementary angles; the acute angles of a right triangle are complementary.

$m \angle I + m \angle R = 90°$; definition of complementary angles.

6. *line 1:* $\overline{ED} \parallel \overline{BC}$; given.

$\angle AED \cong \angle ABC$ and $\angle ADE \cong \angle ACB$; corresponding angles are congruent.

$\triangle ABC \sim \triangle AED$; AA~.

line 2: $\overline{ED} \parallel \overline{BC}$; given.

$\angle B$ and $\angle BED$ are supplementary and $\angle C$ and $\angle CDE$ are supplementary; same side interior angles.

$m \angle C + m \angle CDE = 180°$ and $m \angle B + m \angle BED = 180°$; definition of supplementary angles.

Page 14

1. *line 1:* $m \angle BAC + m \angle CAD + m \angle DAE = m \angle BAE$; angle addition.

$\angle BAC \cong \angle EAD$; given.

$\angle BAC + \angle CAD + \angle BAC = \angle BAE$; substitution.

$2m \angle BAC + m \angle CAD = m \angle BAE$; simplification/multiplication.

line 2: $m \angle BAC + m \angle CAD + m \angle DAE = m \angle BAE$; angle addition.

$\angle BAC \cong \angle EAD$; given.

$m \angle DAE + m \angle CAD + m \angle DAE = m \angle BAE$; substitution.

$2m \angle DAE + m \angle CAD = m \angle BAE$; simplification/multiplication.

line 3: $m \angle BAC + m \angle CAE = m \angle BAE$ and $m \angle BAD + m \angle EAD = m \angle BAE$; angle addition.

$m \angle BAC + m \angle CAE = m \angle BAD + m \angle EAD$; substitution.

$\angle BAC \cong \angle EAD$; given.

$m \angle EAD + m \angle CAE = m \angle BAD + m \angle EAD$; substitution.

$m \angle CAE = m \angle BAD$; subtraction.

2. *line 1:* NKLM is a square; given.

$NK = KL = LM = MN$; definition of a square.

$NL = NL$; reflexive property.

$\triangle NKL \cong \triangle NML$; SSS (the sides of the square and the shared side).

line 2: *NKLM* is a square; given.

    NKLM is a parallelogram; definition of a square.

    $\angle K \cong \angle M$; opposite angles of a parallelogram are congruent.

line 3: *line 2*

    NK = *KL* = *LM* = *MN*; definition of a square.

    $\triangle NKL \cong \triangle NML$; SAS.

line 4: *NKLM* is a square; given.

    $\angle K$ and $\angle M$ are right angles; definition of a square.

    $\triangle NKL$ and $\triangle NML$ are right triangles; definition of a right triangle.

line 5: *NKLM* is a square; given.

    NK = *NM*; definition of a square.

    $\angle K$ and $\angle M$ are right angles; definition of a square.

    NL = *NL*; reflexive property.

    $\triangle NKL \cong \triangle NML$; HL.

3. *line 1:* *X* and *U* are midpoints; given.

    YX = *XW* and *ZU* = *UV*; definition of midpoint.

line 2: *X* and *U* are midpoints; given.

    ZYWV is a trapezoid; definition of a trapezoid.

    $\overline{XU}$ is the median of trapezoid *ZYWV*; definition of median.

    $\overline{XU} \parallel \overline{YZ}$ and $\overline{XU} \parallel \overline{WV}$; the median of a trapezoid is parallel to the bases.

line 3: *line 2*

    $\angle Z$ and $\angle ZUX$ are supplementary and $\angle Y$ and $\angle YXU$ are supplementary; same side interior angles are supplementary.

line 4: *line 2*

    $\angle Y \cong \angle WXU$, $\angle W \cong \angle YXU$, $\angle Z \cong \angle XUV$, $\angle V \cong \angle ZUX$; corresponding angles are congruent.

line 5: *line 2*

    YZUX is a trapezoid and *XWVU* is a trapezoid; definition of a trapezoid.

line 6: *X* and *U* are midpoints; given.

    $\overline{XU}$ is the median of trapezoid *ZYWV*; definition of median.

    $XU = \frac{YZ + WV}{2}$; the length of the median of a trapezoid is the average of the lengths of the bases.

4. *line 1:* $\overline{DE} \parallel \overline{CB}$; given.

   $\angle ADE \cong \angle ACB$ and $\angle AED \cong \angle ABC$; corresponding angles are congruent.

   $\triangle ACB \sim \triangle ADE$; AA $\sim$.

   line 2: $\overline{DE} \parallel \overline{CB}$; given.

   $DEBC$ is a trapezoid; definition of a trapezoid.

   $DEBC$ is a quadrilateral; defintion of a trapezoid.

   The sum of the interior angles of $DEBC$ is $360°$; the sum of the interior angles of a convex polygon is $(n-2)180°$.

   line 3: $\overline{DE} \parallel \overline{CB}$; given.

   $\angle EDC$ and $\angle DCB$ are supplementary and $\angle DEB$ and $\angle CBE$ are supplementary; same side interior angles.

   line 4: line 1

   $\frac{AD}{AC} = \frac{AE}{AB} = \frac{DE}{CB}$; definition of similar triangles.

5. *line 1:* $\overline{DE} \perp \overline{CE}$; given.

   $\angle CED$ is a right angle; definition of perpendicular lines.

   $\triangle CED$ is a right triangle; definition of a right triangle.

   line 2: line 1

   $\angle DCF$ and $\angle CDE$ are complementary angles; the acute angles of a right triangle are complementary.

   $m \angle DCF + m \angle CDE = 90°$; definition of complementary angles.

   line 3: line 1

   $FE = DE$; given.

   $\triangle FED$ is an isosceles right triangle; definition of an isosceles right triangle.

   $m \angle EFD$ and $m \angle EDF$ is $45°$; an isosceles right triangle is a 45–45–90 triangle.

   line 4: $m \angle ACD + m \angle DCF = 180°$; adjacent angles which form a straight angle are supplementary.

   $m \angle ACD = 158°$; given in the picture.

   $158° + m \angle DCF = 180°$; substitution.

   $m \angle DCF = 22°$; subtraction.

   line 5: line 2 + line 4

   $22° + m \angle CDE = 90°$; substitution.

   $m \angle CDE = 68°$.

   line 6: line 5 + line 3 and $m \angle CDE = m \angle CDF + m \angle FDE$; angle addition.

   $68° = m \angle CDF + 45°$; substitution.

   $m \angle CDF = 23°$; subtraction.

6. *line 1:* $\overline{GH} \parallel \overline{IJ}$; given.

    $\angle G \cong \angle J$ and $\angle I \cong \angle H$; alternate interior angles are congruent.

line 2: $\angle GKH \cong \angle IKJ$; vertical angles are congruent

    line 1 (6. *line 1*) above.

    $\Delta GKH \sim \Delta JKI$; AA~.

Page 16

1. Prove: $RS = \frac{1}{2}UV$. If R and S are midpoints of the sides of ΔTUV, then this statement will be true because the segment which connects the midpoints of two sides of a triangle is always half the length of the third side.

2. Prove: $\Delta TRS \sim \Delta TUV$ – AA~ can be used to prove that two triangles are similar if two pairs of angles are congruent. Since they share $\angle T$, that is one pair. So we would need to know that $\angle TRS \cong \angle U$ or $\angle TSR \cong \angle V$. We could know that those angles were congruent if that information were given or if we knew that $\overleftrightarrow{RS} \parallel \overleftrightarrow{UV}$ because then they'd be corresponding angles. We could know that they were parallel if that were given or if we knew that R and S are midpoints because then $\overleftrightarrow{RS}$ would be the segment that connects the midpoints of two sides of the triangle, so it would be parallel to the third side.

3. Prove: $ILJK$ is a parallelogram. If we knew that both pairs of opposite sides were parallel, then the definition of a parallelogram would make this a parallelogram. We could know that the opposite sides were parallel if we knew that $\angle I$ and $\angle IKJ$ were supplementary and that $\angle IKJ$ and $\angle J$ were supplementary because they are same-side interior angles. If we knew that both pairs or opposite sides were congruent, then that would also be information for proving that this is a parallelogram. We could know that the opposite sides were congruent if that information were given or if we knew that $\Delta IKL \cong \Delta JLK$ because then the corresponding parts would be congruent. If we knew that both pairs of opposite angles were congruent, then that would be justification for proving that this was a parallelogram. We would know that the opposite angles were congruent if that information were given or if we knew that the triangles were congruent because then we would have corresponding parts, and we could use angle addition.

4. Prove: $\Delta KIL \cong \Delta LJK$. We can prove that the triangles are congruent based on SAS and based on the fact that opposite sides of a parallelogram are congruent and that opposite angles of a parallelogram are congruent, but then we'd need to know that $ILJK$ is a parallelogram (and all that was discussed in #3). We can prove that the triangles are congruent based on SSS and based on the fact that opposite sides of a parallelogram are congruent and they share $\overline{KL}$, if we know that $ILJK$ is a parallelogram. If we knew that $\angle I \cong \angle J$ and that $\overline{IL} \parallel \overline{KJ}$ based on either given information or $ILJK$ being a parallelogram, then we could deduce that $\angle ILK \cong \angle LKJ$ (alternate interior angles) and we could then use the shared side to prove that the triangles were congruent based on AAS. If we

knew both that $\overline{IL}\|\overline{KJ}$ and that $\overline{IK}\|\overline{JL}$ (either as given information or by knowing that we had a parallelogram), then we could conclude that $\angle ILK \cong \angle LKJ$ and that $\angle IKL \cong \angle KLJ$ based on alternate interior angles. Then using the shared side we could prove that the triangles are congruent based on ASA.

5. Prove: $\overleftrightarrow{DE}$ is tangent to $\odot A$. If we knew that $\overline{AC}\perp\overleftrightarrow{DE}$, then we would know that $\overleftrightarrow{DE}$ was a tangent: A tangent is always perpendicular to the radius at the point of tangency. If that weren't given, we could be told that $\angle ACD$ or $\angle ACE$ was a right angle. If we weren't given that information, if we knew that $\triangle BAC$ was a right triangle, and that $\overline{BA}\|\overrightarrow{DE}$, then we would know that we had the right angles and perpendicular lines we need.

6. Prove: $\triangle ABC$ is 45–45–90 triangle. A 45–45–90 triangle is an isosceles right triangle. We know that $BA = AC$ because all radii of a circle are congruent. We need to be told that $m\angle ABC$ and $m\angle BCA$ are each 45° or that $m\angle BAC = 90°$. Or we could be told that $\overline{BA}\perp\overline{AC}$ so that we could conclude that we had a right angle.

7. Prove: $\triangle MNO \sim \triangle NOP$. There are 3 ways to prove triangles to be similar: AA~, SAS~, and SSS~. In order to use AA~, we need to know that at least 2 pairs of angles are congruent. In order to use SAS~, we need to know the lengths of two pairs of corresponding sides and verify that they are in the same ratio, and the corresponding angles between those sides need to be congruent. In order to use SSS~, we need to know the measures of all of the sides and verify that the corresponding sides are all in the same ratio.

8. Prove: $\angle M \cong \angle P$. If we knew that $\triangle MNO \sim \triangle NOP$, then we would know that the corresponding angles are congruent so we would be able to prove $\angle M \cong \angle P$ (this refers to the discussion in the previous question). If it were given that $\angle MON \cong \angle NPO$ and that $\angle MNO \cong \angle NOP$, then we could use the fact that if two angles of one triangle are congruent to two angles of another triangle, then the third angles of the triangles are congruent.

Pages 18–19

1. Given: $m\angle UZA + m\angle WAZ = 180°$. Prove: $\overleftrightarrow{TZ}\|\overleftrightarrow{AW}$. It's given that $m\angle UZA + m\angle WAZ = 180°$ which means that $\angle UZA$ and $\angle WAZ$ are supplementary angles. Since they are also same-side interior angles, that makes $\overleftrightarrow{TZ}\|\overleftrightarrow{AW}$, because if two lines are cut by a transversal and same-side interior angles are supplementary, then the lines are parallel.

2. Given: $\triangle GKH \cong \triangle JKI$. Prove: $\overline{GH}\|\overline{IJ}$. It's given that $\triangle GKH \cong \triangle JKI$. When two triangles are congruent, then their corresponding parts are congruent, so $\angle G \cong \angle J$. Since $\angle G$ and $\angle J$ are congruent alternate interior angles, that makes $\overline{GH}\|\overline{IJ}$.

3. Given: $\angle OQL \cong \angle SRP$. Prove: $\overleftrightarrow{LM}\|\overleftrightarrow{NS}$. $\angle OQL \cong \angle MQR$ and $\angle SRP \cong \angle QRN$ because vertical angles are congruent. Since it's given that $\angle OQL \cong \angle SRP$, by substitution, $\angle MQR \cong \angle SRP$. Since $\angle MQR$ and $\angle SRP$ are congruent alternate interior angles, $\overleftrightarrow{LM}\|\overleftrightarrow{NS}$.

4. Given: $\overline{AB} \cong \overline{EF}$ and $\overline{AG} \cong \overline{HF}$. Prove: $\overline{GB} \cong \overline{EH}$. Segment addition justifies the statements that $AG + GB = AB$ and that $EH + HF = EF$. Since it is given that $\overline{AB} \cong \overline{EF}$, by substitution, $AG + GB = EF$. Since it is also given that $\overline{AG} \cong \overline{HF}$, by substitution $HF + GB = EF$. By subtraction, $GB = EF - HF$ and $EH = EF - HF$. By substitution, $GB = EH$, so $\overline{GB} \cong \overline{EH}$.

5. Given: $\overrightarrow{QR} \perp \overrightarrow{QP}$ and $m\angle TQR + m\angle SQP = 90°$. Prove: $m\angle TQR = m\angle RQS$. Since it is given that $\overrightarrow{QR} \perp \overrightarrow{QP}$, based on the definition of perpendicular lines, $\angle RQP$ is a right angle. Based on the definition of a right angle, $m\angle RQP = 90°$. Angle addition justifies the statement that $m\angle RQS + m\angle SQP = m\angle RQP = 90°$. It is also given that $m\angle TQR + m\angle SQP = 90°$. By subtraction, $m\angle RQS = 90° - m\angle SQP$ and $m\angle TQR = 90° - m\angle SQP$. So by substitution, $m\angle TQR = m\angle RQS$.

Pages 20–21

1. It is given that $\overline{CG} \perp \overline{AE}$, so the definition of perpendicular lines allows us to conclude that $\angle CIA$ and $\angle CIE$ are both right angles. The definition of right angles allows us to conclude that $m\angle CIA = m\angle CIE = 90°$. It is also given that I is the midpoint of $\overline{AE}$. Based on the definition of a midpoint, $AI = IE$. Since $\triangle AIC$ and $\triangle EIC$ share $\overline{CI}$, $\triangle AIC \cong \triangle EIC$ by SAS.

2. Since it is given that $\triangle JNO$ is equiangular, $m\angle J = m\angle N = m\angle O = 60°$ by the definition of an equiangular triangle. Since it is given that $LKOM$ is a parallelogram, and we know that consecutive angles of a parallelogram are supplementary, $m\angle OKL$ is 120° because $m\angle O = 60°$. However, $\angle OKL$ and $\angle JKL$ are also supplementary because they form straight angles, so $m\angle JKL = 60°$. If $m\angle J = 60°$ and $m\angle JKL = 60°$, then $m\angle JLK$ must also be 60° because the sum of the interior angles of a triangle is 180°. That makes $\triangle JLK$ an equiangular triangle by definition. Since all equiangular triangles are also equilateral, $\triangle JLK$ is an equilateral triangle. Note: there are many good ways to do this proof including using rules about the base angles of an isosceles triangle and the fact that the opposite sides of a parallelogram are congruent.

3. Since it is given that $\triangle ADE \sim \triangle ACB$, we know that the angles of $\triangle ADE$ are congruent to the corresponding angles of $\triangle ACB$. Therefore $\angle ADE \cong \angle ACB$ and $\angle AED \cong \angle ABC$. They are pairs of corresponding angles which are congruent, which makes $\overline{DE} \parallel \overline{BC}$.

4. $\triangle ABC$ is an isosceles triangle by definition because it is given that $\overline{AC} \cong \overline{BC}$. Therefore $\angle BAC \cong \angle ABC$ because the base angles of an isosceles triangle are congruent. By angle addition, $m\angle BAC = m\angle BAD + m\angle DAC$ and $m\angle ABC = m\angle DBA + m\angle CBD$. However, it is given that $\angle BAD \cong \angle DBA$. Therefore, by substitution, $m\angle BAC = m\angle DBA + m\angle DAC$. Also by substitution, $m\angle BAC = m\angle DBA + m\angle CBD$. By subtraction, $m\angle DAC = m\angle CBD$.

5. Since it is given that $\overleftrightarrow{EI}$ and $\overrightarrow{DH}$ are both tangent to $\odot A$, they are each perpendicular to the radius they meet at their points of tangency. But the points of tangency are the endpoints of the diameter, so $\overleftrightarrow{EI} \perp \overline{ED}$ and $\overleftrightarrow{DH} \perp \overline{ED}$. When two lines are perpendicular to the same line, they are parallel to each other, so $\overleftrightarrow{EI} \| \overleftrightarrow{DH}$. It is also given that $\angle EIG$ is a right angle, so $\overleftrightarrow{EI} \perp \overleftrightarrow{IH}$ by the definition of perpendicular lines. Since $\overleftrightarrow{EI}$ is perpendicular to both $\overleftrightarrow{IH}$ and $\overleftrightarrow{ED}$, $\overleftrightarrow{IH} \| \overleftrightarrow{ED}$. Both pairs of opposite sides of quadrilateral *DEIH* are parallel, so it is a parallelogram. When a parallelogram contains one right angle, it contains 4 right angles, so parallelogram *DEIH* is a rectangle.

Page 23

1. *Proof 1:* $\angle YZU$ and $\angle WVU$ are right angles according to the given. Therefore by the definition of perpendicular lines, $\overline{YZ}$ and $\overline{WV}$ are both perpendicular to $\overline{ZV}$. When two lines are perpendicular to the same line, they are parallel to each other, so $\overline{YZ} \| \overline{WV}$. A trapezoid is a quadrilateral with exactly one pair of opposite sides which are congruent, so *YZVW* is a trapezoid. Since it is given that *X* and *U* are midpoints, by the definition of a median of a trapezoid, $\overline{XU}$ is a median. The median of a trapezoid is always parallel to the bases, so $\overline{XU} \| \overline{WV}$. By the definition of a trapezoid, *WVUX* is a trapezoid.

    Proof 2: It is given that $\angle YZU$ and $\angle WVU$ are both right angles, so they each have a measure of 90° by the definition of right angles. 90° + 90° = 180°, so $\angle YZU$ and $\angle WVU$ are supplementary angles by definition. When same-side interior angles are supplementary, the lines are parallel, so $\overline{YZ} \| \overline{WV}$. A trapezoid is a quadrilateral with exactly one pair of opposite sides which are congruent, so *YZVW* is a trapezoid. Since it is given that *X* and *U* are midpoints, by the definition of a median of a trapezoid, $\overline{XU}$ is a median. The median of a trapezoid is always parallel to the bases, so $\overline{XU} \| \overline{WV}$. By the definition of a trapezoid, *WVUX* is a trapezoid.

2. *Proof 1:* Since it is given that $\overline{JK} \| \overline{LM}$, alternate interior angles are congruent, which means that $\angle J \cong \angle M$ and $\angle L \cong \angle K$. It is also given that $\overline{JK} \cong \overline{LM}$. $\overline{JK}$ is the included side for $\angle J$ and $\angle K$, and $\overline{LM}$ is the included side for $\angle L$ and $\angle M$. By ASA, $\triangle JKN \cong \triangle MLN$.

    Proof 2: $\angle JNK \cong \angle MNL$ because vertical angles are congruent. It is given that $\overline{JK}$ and $\overline{LM}$ are both congruent and parallel. Therefore $\angle J$ and $\angle M$ are congruent because they are alternate interior angles. So $\triangle JKN \cong \triangle MLN$ by AAS.

3. *Proof 1:* The given information is that *JHIK* is a square. A square has 4 congruent sides, so *JH* = *HI* = *IK* = *KJ*. The diagonals of a square are congruent, so *JI* = *HK*. The diagonals of a square also bisect each other, so *JF* = *FI* and *HF* = *KF*. Using segment addition and some simplification, *JF* + *FI* = 2*JF* = *JI* and *HF* + *KF* = 2*KF* = *HK*. By substitution, 2*JF* = 2*KF*, and by division, *JF* = *KF*. Using the same process, you can show that *HF* = *FI*. Therefore, $\triangle JFH \cong \triangle KFI$, by SSS.

Proof 2: We are told that *JHIK* is a square. Since a square is a rectangle, it has 4 right angles. Since a square is a rhombus, the diagonals bisect the angles, so each corner has two 45° angles. △*JFH* and △*KFI*, therefore, are both isosceles triangles with base angles of 45°. The sides of a square are congruent, so we know that $\overline{JH} \cong \overline{KI}$. By ASA, △*JFH* ≅ △*KFI*.

Note: You can't use alternate interior angles to say that ∠HJF ≅ ∠FIK and that ∠FKI ≅ ∠FHJ because of the way the triangles are named. These are not corresponding angles in the triangles as named so the congruencies are not helpful.

Pages 25–27

1. Order — Reason:

   a. 3 — Substitution; b. 4 —Given; c. 2 — Given; d. 6 — Subtraction; e. 1 — Segment addition; f. 5 — Substitution.

2. Order — Reason:

   a. 3 —AA~; b. 1 — Given; c. 2—When parallel lines are cut by a transversal, alternate interior angles are congruent.

3. Order — Reason:

   a. 6 — Given; b. 3 — Definition of a right angle; c. 5 — Substitution; d. 7 — Substitution; e. 4 — Angle addition; f. 1 — Given; g. 2 — Definition of a perpendicular line; h. 8 — Subtraction.

4. Order — Reason: *Only one option is presented for this proof. Other options are possible.*

   a. 4 — Definition of a right angle; b. 7 — Given; c. 10 — Definition of a cosine; d. 14 — The acute angles of a right triangle are complementary; e. 18 — Definition of a 30–60–90 triangle; f. 1 — Given; g. 5 — Given ; h. 6 — Midpoint theorem; i. 8 — Substitution; j. 3 — Definition of a perpendicular line; k. 16 — Substitution; l. 13 — Substitution and simplification; m. 11 — Substitution; n. 15 — Definition of complementary angles; o. 17 — Subtraction; p. 12 — Definition of *cos* 60° (table of values or calculator); q. 2 — A tangent is perpendicular to the radii at the point of tangency; r. 9 — Division.

5. Order — Reason:

   a. 6 — SAS; b. 9 — Substitution; c. 1 — Given; d. 3 — Reflexive property; e. 12 — Subtraction; f. 7 — Angle addition; g. 7 —Angle addition; h. 11 — Substitution; i. 2 — Definition of a segment bisector; j. 5 — All right angles are congruent; k. 4 — Definition of a perpendicular line; l. 10 — CPCTC; m. 8— CPCTC.

Pages 28–29

1. Given: ⊙H; points I, J and K are on the circle; $m \angle J = 45°$.

   Prove: $\triangle IKJ$ is an isosceles triangle.

Statement	Reasons
1. ⊙H; points I, J and K are on the circle.	1. Given
2. $\overline{IJ}$ is a diameter.	2. Definition of a diameter
3. $\overparen{IKJ}$ is a semicircle.	3. Definition of semicircle
4. $\angle IKJ$ is a right angle.	4. If an angle is inscribed in a semicircle, then it is a right angle.
5. $\triangle IJK$ is a right triangle.	5. Definition of a right triangle
6. $\angle I$ and $\angle J$ are complementary.	6. Acute angles of right triangles are complementary.
7. $m \angle I + m \angle J = 90°$	7. Definition of complementary angles
8. $m \angle J = 45°$	8. Given
9. $m \angle I + 45° = 90°$	9. Substitution
10. $m \angle I = 45°$	10. Subtraction
11. $\overline{IK} \cong \overline{JK}$	11. If two angles of a triangle are congruent, then the sides opposite those angles are congruent.
12. $\triangle IKJ$ is an isosceles triangle.	12. Definition of an isosceles triangle

2. Given: $\angle MQN \cong \angle OTR$.

   Prove: $\overleftrightarrow{SN} \| \overleftrightarrow{OP}$.

Statements	Reasons
1. $\angle MQN$ and $\angle NQT$ are supplementary. $\angle OTR$ and $\angle OTQ$ are supplementary.	1. Adjacent angles that form a straight angle are supplementary.
2. $\angle MQN \cong \angle OTR$	2. Given
3. $\angle NQT \cong \angle OTQ$	3. Supplements of congruent angles are congruent.
4. $\overleftrightarrow{SN} \| \overleftrightarrow{OP}$	4. Alternate interior angles

3. Given: $\triangle BEC \cong \triangle DEA$;

   Prove: E is the midpoint of $\overline{AC}$.

Statements	Reasons
1. $\triangle BEC \cong \triangle DEA$	1. Given
2. $\angle CBE \cong \angle ADE$ (or $\angle BCE \cong \angle DAE$)	2. CPCTC
3. $\overline{CB} \| \overline{AD}$	3. Alternate interior angles.
4. $\overline{BC} \cong \overline{AD}$	4. CPCTC
5. $ABCD$ is a parallelogram.	5. If one pair of opposite sides of a quadrilateral are both congruent and parallel, then the quadrilateral is a parallelogram.

6. $\overline{AC}$ bisects $\overline{BD}$ (or $\overline{BD}$ bisects $\overline{AC}$ or $\overline{AC}$ and $\overline{BD}$ bisect each other).	6. The diagonals of a parallelogram bisect each other.
7. E is the midpoint of $\overline{AC}$.	7. Definition of a segment bisector

4. Given: $\triangle PQR \cong \triangle TSR$.
   Prove: $\triangle PQS \cong \triangle TSQ$.

Statements	Reasons
1. $\triangle PQR \cong \triangle TSR$.	1. Given
2. $\angle P \cong \angle T$; $\angle PQR \cong \triangle TSR$; $\overline{QR} \cong \overline{RS}$; $\overline{PQ} \cong \overline{TS}$	2. CPCTC
3. $\triangle QRS$ is an isosceles triangle.	3. Definition of an isosceles triangle
4. $\angle RQS \cong \angle RSQ$	4. Base angles of an isosceles triangle are congruent.
5. $\angle PQR + \angle RQS \cong \angle TSR + \angle RSQ$	5. Addition
6. $\angle PQR + \angle RQS \cong \angle PQS$ and $\angle TSR + \angle RSQ \cong \angle TSQ$	6. Angle Addition
7. $\angle PQS \cong \angle TSQ$	7. Substitution
8. $\triangle PQS \cong \triangle TSQ$	8. ASA

5. Given: trapezoid $UVXY$; W and Z are midpoints.
   Prove: $WZUV$ is a trapezoid.

Statements	Reasons
1. Trapezoid $UVXY$; W and Z are midpoints.	1. Given
2. $\overline{WZ}$ is a median.	2. Definition of median
3. $\overline{WZ} \parallel \overline{VU}$	3. Median of a trapezoid is parallel to the bases.
4. $WZUV$ is a trapezoid.	4. Definition of trapezoid

Pages 32–33

It is possible that there are other correct ways to do the proofs in Strategy 6. If you're wondering, check with a teacher, friend, etc.

1.
Statements	Reasons
1. $\triangle ACE$ and $\triangle AGE$ are isosceles triangles with $\overline{AE}$ as their base.	1. Given
2. $\overline{AC} \cong \overline{CE}$; $\overline{AG} \cong \overline{GE}$	2. Definition of isosceles triangle
3. $ACEG$ is a kite.	3. Definition of kite

2.
Statements	Reasons
1. $\overline{AD} \parallel \overline{BC}$	1. Given
2. $\angle DAB \cong \angle ABC$; $\angle EAC \cong \angle ACB$	2. Alternate interior angles
3. $\angle DAB \cong \angle EAC$	3. Given
4. $\angle ABC \cong \angle ACB$	4. Substitution

| 5. $\overline{AB} \cong \overline{AC}$ | 5. If 2 angles of a triangle are congruent, then the sides opposite those angles are congruent. |
| 6. $\triangle ABC$ is an isosceles triangle. | 6. Definition of an isosceles triangle |

Note: You could put all of the givens together in the first statement. The approach used here is only to include the given when it becomes necessary to include it in order to proceed.

3.
Statements	Reasons
1. V and W are midpoints.	1. Given
2. $RV = VS$	2. Definition of midpoint
3. $RV + VS = RS$	3. Segment addition
4. $RV + RV = RS$	4. Substitution
5. $2RV = RS$	5. Simplication
6. $RU = RV$	6. Given
7. $2RU = RS$	7. Substitution

Note: Sometimes information is given that is not needed. In this instance, W as a midpoint is not necessary information and could have been left out.

4.
Statements	Reasons
1. $\angle BAC \cong \angle EAD$	1. Given
2. $\angle BAC + \angle CAD \cong \angle BAD$; $\angle EAD + \angle CAD \cong \angle CAE$	2. Angle addition
3. $\angle CAD \cong \angle BAD - \angle BAC$; $\angle CAD \cong \angle CAE - \angle EAD$.	3. Subtraction
4. $\angle BAD - \angle BAC \cong \angle CAE - \angle EAD$	4. Transitive
5. $\angle BAD - \angle BAC \cong \angle CAE - \angle BAC$	5. Substitution
6. $\angle BAD \cong \angle CAE$	6. Addition

Note: There are other ways to manipulate the equations from step 2 using addition, subtraction and substitution to get to step 6 that are equally valid.

5.
Statements	Reasons
1. $\angle BAD$ and $\angle ADC$ are right angles.	1. Given
2. $m\angle BAD = 90°$; $m\angle ADC = 90°$	2. Definition of a right angle
3. $90° + 90° = 180°$	3. Addition
4. $m\angle BAD + m\angle ADC = 180°$	4. Substitution
5. $\angle BAD$ and $\angle ADC$ are supplementary.	5. Definition of supplementary angles
6. $\overline{AB} \| \overline{EC}$	6. Same-side interior angles
7. $EABC$ is a trapezoid.	7. Definition of a trapezoid

Page 34–35

There are other correct ways to do these proofs. If you're wondering, check with a teacher, friend, etc.

1.
Statements	Reasons
1. $\overline{LM} \cong \overline{MJ}$; $\overline{LI} \cong \overline{IK}$	1. Given
2. M and I are midpoints.	2. Definition of midpoint
3. $\overline{MI}$ is the midpoint connector.	3. Definition of midpoint connector

4. $\overline{MI} \parallel \overline{JK}$	4. The midpoint connector is parallel to the third side.
5. $\angle MIK$ and $\angle JKI$ are supplementary.	5. Same-side interior angles
6. $m\angle MIK + m\angle JKI = 180°$	6. Definition of supplementary angles

2.

Statements	Reasons
1. $\angle JAK \cong \angle ADE \cong \angle GBF$	1. Given
2. $\overleftrightarrow{AB} \parallel \overleftrightarrow{DE}$; $\overleftrightarrow{BE} \parallel \overleftrightarrow{AD}$	2. Corresponding angles.
3. $ABED$ is a parallelogram.	3. Definition of parallelogram.

3. *There are a variety of other correct ways to organize the steps.*

Statements	Reasons
1. I and F are midpoints on parallelogram $EGJH$.	1. Given
2. $\overline{EI} \cong \overline{IG}$; $\overline{HF} \cong \overline{FJ}$	2. Definition of midpoint
3. $EI + IG = EG$; $HF + FJ = HJ$	3. Segment addition
4. $EI + EI = EG$; $HF + HF = HJ$	4. Substitution
5. $2EI = EG$; $2HF = HJ$	5. Simplification
6. $\overline{EG} \cong \overline{HJ}$; $\overline{EH} \cong \overline{GJ}$	6. Opposite sides of a parallelogram are congruent.
7. $2EI = 2HF$	7. Substitution
8. $EI = HF$	8. Division
9. $\overline{IF} \cong \overline{IG}$	9. Given
10. $EI = IF$	10. Substitution
11. $\overline{FJ} \cong \overline{GJ}$	11. Given
12. $GJ = HF = IF = EH$	12. Substitution
13. $EIFH$ is a rhombus.	13. Definition of a rhombus

4.

Statements	Reasons
1. $\triangle WXY \cong \triangle YZW$	1. Given
2. $\overline{XY} \cong \overline{WZ}$; $\overline{XW} \cong \overline{YZ}$	2. CPCTC
3. $XYZW$ is a parallelogram.	3. Both pairs of opposite sides are congruent.
4. $XY^2 + XW^2 = WY^2$	4. Given
5. $\triangle XWY$ is a right triangle.	5. Pythagorean Theorem (its converse)
6. $\angle WXY$ is a right angle.	6. Definition of a right triangle
7. $\angle YZW$ is a right angle.	7. CPCTC
8. $\overline{XY} \parallel \overline{WZ}$	8. Definition of a parallelogram
9. $\angle YXW$ and $\angle XWZ$ are supplementary; $\angle XYZ$ and $\angle YZW$ are supplementary.	9. Same-side interior angles
10. $\angle XWZ \cong \angle XYZ$	10. Supplements of congruent angles are congruent.

5. | Statements | Reasons |
|---|---|
| 1. *GIJF* is a trapezoid. | 1. Given |
| 2. $\overline{FJ}\parallel\overline{GI}$ or $\overline{FJ}\parallel\overline{GH}$ | 2. Definition of a trapezoid |
| 3. $m\angle HJI + m\angle HIJ = m\angle JHG$ | 3. The sum of the two remote interior angles of a triangle is equal to the measure of the exterior angle. |
| 4. $m\angle HJI + m\angle HIJ = m\angle F$ | 4. Given |
| 5. $m\angle F \cong m\angle JHG$ | 5. Substitution |
| 6. $\angle F$ and $\angle G$ are supplementary. $\angle FJH$ and $\angle JHG$ are supplementary. | 6. Same-side interior angles are supplementary when a transversal cuts a pair of parallel lines. |
| 7. $\angle G \cong \angle FJH$ | 7. Supplements of congruent angles are congruent. |
| 8. *FGHJ* is a parallelogram. | 8. Both pairs of opposite angles are congruent. |

Page 36–37

There are other correct ways to do these proofs. If you're wondering, check with a teacher, friend, etc.

1. | Statements | Reasons |
|---|---|
| 1. *STUV* is a parallelogram. | 1. Given |
| 2. $\angle V \cong \angle T$ | 2. Opposite angles of a parallelogram are congruent. |
| 3. $\overline{ST}\parallel\overline{VU}$ | 3. Definition of a parallelogram |
| 4. $\angle TSU \cong \angle SUV$ | 4. Alternate interior angles |
| 5. $\overline{SU} \cong \overline{SU}$ | 5. Reflexive |
| 6. $\triangle VSU \cong \triangle TUS$ | 6. AAS |

Statements	Reasons
1. *STUV* is a parallelogram.	1. Given
2. $\overline{ST} \cong \overline{VU}$; $\overline{VS} \cong \overline{TU}$	2. Opposite sides of a parallelogram are congruent.
3. $\overline{SU} \cong \overline{SU}$	3. Reflexive
4. $\triangle VSU \cong \triangle TUS$	4. SSS

2. | Statements | Reasons |
|---|---|
| 1. $\angle I \cong \angle E$ | 1. Given. |
| 2. $\overline{AI} \cong \overline{AE}$ | 2. If 2 angles of a triangle are congruent, then the sides opposite those angles are congruent. |
| 3. *O* is a midpoint. | 3. Given |
| 4. $\overline{IO} \cong \overline{OE}$ | 4. Definition of midpoint |
| 5. $\triangle AIO \cong \triangle AEO$ | 5. SAS |
| 6. $\angle IAO \cong \angle EAO$ | 6. CPCTC |

Statements	Reasons
1. $\angle I \cong \angle E$	1. Given
2. $\overline{AI} \cong \overline{AE}$	2. If 2 angles of a triangle are congruent, then the sides opposite those angles are congruent.
3. $\triangle AIE$ is isosceles.	3. Definition of an isosceles triangle
4. O is a midpoint; $\angle AOE$ is a right angle.	4. Given
5. $\overline{AO}$ is a perpendicular bisector.	5. Definition of perpendicular bisector
6. $\overline{AO}$ is the bisector of $\angle IAE$.	6. In an isosceles triangle, the perpendicular bisector of the base is also the angle bisector of the vertex angle.
7. $\angle IAO \cong \angle EAO$	7. Definition of an angle bisector